VERY BRITISH
TODDLER KNITS

25 classic designs for 1 to 6 year olds

A QUAIL PUBLISHING TITLE

Published in 2018 by
Search Press Ltd
Wellwood
North Farm Road
Tunbridge Wells
Kent, TN2 3DR
UK

ISBN: 978-1-78221-552-3

Conceived, designed and produced by
Quail Publishing
Office 10, The Incuba,
1 Brewers Hill Road,
Bedfordshire, LU6 1AA

Pattern Checking: Deb Bramham
Art Editor: Georgina Brant
Designers: Quail Studio
Photographer: Jarek Duk
Models: Eliza-Rose Gardner, Charles Luckins
Illustration: Susan Campbell
Publisher: Quail Publishing
Yarn Support: Rowan Yarns, Rooster Yarns & Millamia

Printed in China

I dedicate this book to:
Bernard Grant Campbell
& Marcel Oscar Raccommandato

VERY BRITISH
TODDLER KNITS

25 classic designs for 1 to 6 year olds

Susan Campbell

SEARCH PRESS

Contents

Project Gallery

Glamis Cabled Cardigan
page 18

Glamis Garter Stitch Cardigan
page 22

Glamis Hat
page 24

Glamis Long-Sleeved Dress
page 26

Hampton Jumper
page 36

Hampton Hat
page 40

Hampton Cardigan
page 42

Hampton Mouse Scarf
page 46

Hampton Mouse Rucksack
page 48

Kensington Butterfly Jumper
page 60

**Kensington Cross-over
Cardigan** *page 64*

**Kensington Garter Stitch
Cross-over Cardigan** *page 70*

Project Gallery Cont.

Kensington Headband
page 72

Kensington Dress
page 74

Holyrood Cabled Sweater
page 82

Holyrood Gilet
page 88

Holyrood Hat
page 96

Holyrood Scarf
page 98

Toy Mice
page 100

Mice Clothes
page 106

INTRODUCTION

I live and work in a wonderful valley in northwest Norfolk, an area rather grandly known as the Royal Coast. Our estate borders on the Royal Sandringham Estate, the country home and traditional Christmas retreat of HRH Queen Elizabeth II and her family. Recently we were delighted to welcome yet more royal neighbours; the Duke and Duchess of Cambridge have refurbished Anmer Hall, which is even closer to us than Sandringham House. *Very British Toddler Knits* has been designed with the new generation of royal children very much in mind.

Being a mother of six, stepmother of two, grandmother of nine and step-grandmother of ten, I count myself an expert in the grandmother world, and more importantly a veteran in the design of baby clothes. I've been designing small person's knitwear for a very long time – no design of mine will have to be squeezed over a child's head and no baby will have to be stripped almost naked to facilitate a nappy change.

My childrens knitwear designs have travelled far – from angel tops to tank tops, from cot blankets to sleep-bags, from knitted lace to contemporary chunky – a journey that I have enjoyed every stitch of the way.

My new collection is unashamedly based on classic British design, which is never boring, never outdated and never fussy, with the added bonus that the designs are quick and easy knit.

I hope you enjoy knitting my designs for your little one.

Susan Campbell x

Glamis

In 1372, Sir John Lyon was granted the thanage of Glamis by King Robert II of Scotland for services rendered to the crown. He later married the King's daughter, Princess Joanna. It is from this union that the much loved Elizabeth Bowes Lyon, later to become the Queen Mother, descends. Glamis was the childhood home of the Queen Mother and was always very close to her heart.

The Glamis Collection is knitted in subtle heather tones, echoing the hues of the landscape surrounding Glamis. Slightly retro prints have been used to edge and embellish the garments, a fond reminder of the era in with the Queen Mother lived.

Cardigan

Cabled Version

ABBREVIATIONS

C2B – cable two back – slip next 2 sts onto a cable needle
and hold at back of the work, K2, K2 from cable needle.

C2F – cable two front – slip next 2 sts onto a cable
needle and hold at front of the work, K2, K2 from cable
needle.

FRONT LEFT SIDE

With 4mm (US 6) needles, cast on 31(33,35) sts.
K 2 rows.
Row 1 K to last 10 sts, P2, K4, P2, K2.
Row 2 P2, K2, P4, K2, P to end.
Row 3 K to last 10 sts, P2, C2B, P2, K2.
Row 4 As Row 2.
Row 5 As Row 1.
Row 6 As Row 2.
These 6 rows set pattern.
Rep Rows 1–6 11(12,13) times more, ending the final
rep on Row 5. 71(77,83) rows of cable pattern have been
worked in total. (You can adjust the length here, but
ensure you still end on Row 5.)

Sleeve
Next row (WS) P2, K2, P4, K2, P to end, cast on 20 sts.
51(53,55) sts
Row 1 K2, P2, K4, P2, K to last 10 sts, P2, K4, P2, K2.

Row 2 P2, K2, P4, K2, P to last 10 sts, K2, P4, K2, P2.
Row 3 K2, P2, C2B, P2, K to last 10 sts, P2, C2B,
P2, K2.

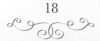

Row 4 As Row 2.
Row 5 As Row 1.
Row 6 As Row 2.
These 6 rows set pattern.
Keeping front and sleeve edging correct, work another 20 rows in pattern established.

Row 27 (RS) P2, K2, P4, K2, P to last 10 sts, leave last 10 sts (front edge) on a stitch holder.
Row 28 P to last 10 sts, K2, P4, K2, P2.
Row 29 K2, P2, K4, P2, K to last 2 sts, K2tog (neck edge). *40(42,44) sts*
Row 30 P2tog, P to last 10 sts, K2, P4, K2, P2. *39(41,43) sts*
Row 31 As Row 29. *38(40,42) sts*
Row 32 As Row 30. *37(39,41) sts*
Row 33 K2, P2, C2B, P2, K to end.
Cont working the cable at the sleeve edge.
Work 7 rows straight, ending on a WS row.
Slip remaining sts onto a stitch holder.

FRONT RIGHT SIDE

With 4mm (US 6) needles, cast on 31(33,35)sts.
K 2 rows.
Row 1 K2, P2, K4, P2, K to end.
Row 2 P to last 10 sts, K2, P4, K2, P2.
Row 3 K2, P2, C2F, P2, K to end.
Row 4 As Row 2.
Row 5 As Row 1.
Row 6 As Row 2.
These 6 rows set pattern.
Rep Rows 1–6 11(12,13) times more, ending the final rep on Row 5. 71(77,83) rows of cable pattern have been worked in total. (If you adjusted the length on the left front, work the same number of repeats here, but ensure you still end on Row 5.)

Sleeve

Next row (WS) Cast on 20 sts, P to last 10 sts, K2, P4, K2, P2. *51(53,55) sts*
Row 1 K2, P2, K4, P2, K to last 10 sts, P2, K4, P2, K2.
Row 2 P2, K2, P4, K2, P to last 10 sts, K2, P4, K2, P2.
Row 3 K2, P2, C2F, P2, K to last 10 sts, P2, C2F, P2, K2.
Row 4 As Row 2.
Row 5 As Row 1.
Row 6 As Row 2.
These 6 rows set pattern.

Keeping front and sleeve edging correct, work another 21 rows in pattern established.
Row 28 P2, K2, P4, K2, P to last 10 sts, leave last 10 sts (front edge) on a stitch holder. *41(43,45) sts*
Row 29 Skpo, K to last 10 sts, P2, K4, P2, K2. *40(42,44) sts*
Row 30 P2, K2, P4, K2, P to last 2 sts, P2tog tbl. *39(41,43) sts*
Row 31 As Row 29. *38(40,42) sts*
Row 32 As Row 30. *37(39,41) sts*
Row 33 K to last 10 sts, P2, C2F, P2, K2.
Cont working the cable at the sleeve edge.
Work 7 rows straight, ending on a WS row.
Slip remaining sts onto a stitch holder.

BACK

Keeping the cable pattern on the sleeve edge correct, K across left front 37(39,41) sts, cast on 28 sts, K across right front 37(39,41) sts keeping second cable correct. *102(106,110) sts*
Work 39 rows.
Cast off 20 sts at beg of next 2 rows. *62(66,70) sts*
Work 68(74,80) rows in st st. (If you adjusted the length on the front pieces, remember to adjust the back length to match.)
K 2 rows.
Cast off.

NECK BAND

Slip the 10 sts from the top of the left front cable band onto a needle.
Work the 10 cable sts until the band reaches the centre neck back.
Cast off.
Rep for right side neck band.

TO MAKE UP

Block and press work.
Beg 3cm/1¼in from the bottom edge, join the side seams and then the sleeve seams.
Join the band at the back of neck.
Slip stitch the band into place.

Side slits

With RS facing and beg at the bottom edge, pick up and K into every st.
Cast off.
Rep on slide slit on other seam.

Front button band

Cast on 14 sts.

Work 13(24,25)cm/5(9½,9¾)in in K1, P1 moss st.

Make 3 I-cords for the button loops.

To make an I-cord

Using 4mm (US 6) double-pointed needles, cast on
4 sts.

K to end of row.

*Slide the sts to the right-hand side of the needle.

Pull yarn taut and K another row. *

Rep from * to * until the I-cord is 10cm/4in long.

K4tog and fasten off.

Form each I-cord into a loop and sew the ends to the
inside edge of the right-hand cable border.

Using slip st, sew the moss st band to the inside of
the left-hand front, fixing it to the inside edge of the
cable border. Then fix it to the outside edge of the
cable border from the top down as far as the bottom
button loop.

Sew the buttons into place.

Cardigan

Garter Stitch Version

You will need

SIZE
1–2(2–3,3–4) years

Actual chest circumference:
59(63,66.5)cm/23¼(24¾, 21¼)in

YARN
Rooster *Almerino DK (Grape)*
4(5,5) x 50g/1¾oz balls

NEEDLES
Pair of 4mm (US 6) knitting needles

EXTRAS
Stitch holders
Buttons: 1 x 22mm/¾in button
for covering
Bias binding: approx. 120cm/47in

TENSION
21 sts and 28 rows to 10cm/4in square
over st st using 4mm (US 6) needles

NOTE
Pattern is worked in garter st throughout.

FRONT LEFT SIDE
With 4mm (US 6) needles, cast on 31(33,35) sts.
Work in garter st until front measures
25(27.5,30)cm/9¾(10¾,11¾)in, ending on a WS row.

Sleeve
Next row Cast on 18 sts, K to end. *49(51,53) sts*
Work straight until sleeve measures 10cm/4in, ending on
a WS row.
Row 1 K to last 12 sts (neck edge), K2tog, K to end of
row. *48(50,52) sts*
Row 2 K10, K2tog, K to end. *47(49,51) sts*
Row 3 As Row 1. *46(48,50) sts*
Row 4 As Row 2. *45(47,49) sts*
Row 5 As Row 1. *44(46,48) sts*
Work straight until sleeve measures 13cm/5in, ending on
a WS row.
Slip remaining sts onto a stitch holder.

FRONT RIGHT SIDE
Work as for left side, reversing shaping.

BACK
With RS facing, beg at sleeve edge, K34(36,38) sts across
left front sts, slip next 10 sts onto a stitch holder, cast on
28 sts, slip first 10 sts of the right neck onto a stitch holder,
K34(36,38) sts across right front sts.

Work straight on these 96(100,104) sts until the back sleeves measure the same the front sleeves.
Cast off 18 sts at beg of next 2 rows. *60(64,68) sts*
Work straight until the back measures the same as the fronts.
Cast off.

NECK BAND

Slip the 10 sts from the top of the left front band onto a needle.
Work in garter st until the band reaches the centre neck back.
Cast off.
Rep for right side neck band.

TO MAKE UP

Block and press work.
Join the side and sleeve seams.
Join the band at the back of neck.
Slip stitch the band into place.
Make 1 I-cord for the button loop as for the cabled gilet.
Sew the loop into place (see page 123).
With RSs facing, sew the bias binding all around the front and neck edge. Fold the bias binding to the inside and slip st into position.
Cover the button (see page 120) and sew into place.
Add fabric band along back neck if desired (see page 121).

Hat

With Ear Flaps

You will need

SIZE
1–2(2–3,3–4) years

YARN
Rooster *Almerino DK*
1 x 50g/1¾oz ball in main colour *(Grape)*
Small amount in contrast colour *(Lilac Sky)*
for bow and plaits

NEEDLES
Pair of 4mm (US 6) knitting needles
1 double-pointed needle

TENSION
21 sts and 28 rows to 10cm/4in square
over st st using 4mm (US 6) needles

EAR FLAPS (make 2)
With 4mm (US 6) needles, cast on 7(9,9) sts.
Row 1 (RS) M1 into first st, moss st to last 2 sts, M1 into
next st, work 1 st. *9(11,11) sts*
Rep Row 1 twice more. *13(15,15) sts*
Row 2 Moss st to end.
Rep Rows 1 and 2 until there are 19(21,23) sts.
Cont straight in moss st until ear flap measures 7(8,9)cm
/2¾(3¼,3½)in from beg, ending on a WS row.
Slip first ear flap onto the double-pointed needle and
work the second ear flap.

HEAD SECTION
With 4mm (US 6) needles, cast on 4(6,10) sts, moss st
19(21,23) sts from the second ear flap, cast on 26(30,34)
sts, moss st 19(21,23) sts from the first ear flat ensuring
that the moss st continues correctly, cast on 6 sts.
74(84,96) sts
Work 10 rows in moss st.
Work in st st until the hat measures
10(11,12)cm/4(4¼,4¾)in from the beg of the
head section.

Shape Crown
Row 1 K5(8,10), *K2tog, K2tog tbl, K16(17,20),* rep
from * to * twice more, K2tog, K2tog tbl, K5(9,10).
66(76,88) sts
Row 2 and every alt row P.
Row 3 K4(7,9), *K2tog, K2tog tbl, K14(15,18),* rep from
* to * twice more, K2tog, K2tog tbl, K4(8,9). *58(68,80) sts*

Row 5 K3(6,8), *K2tog, K2tog tbl, K12(13,16),* rep from * to * twice more, K2tog, K2tog tbl, K3(7,8). *50(60,72) sts*

Row 7 K2(5,7), *K2tog, K2tog tbl, K10(11,14),* rep from * to * twice more, K2tog, K2tog tbl, K2(6,7). *42(52,64) sts*

Row 9 K1(4,6), *K2tog, K2tog tbl, K8(9,12),* rep from * to * twice more, K2tog, K2tog tbl, K1(5,6). *34(44,56) sts*

Row 11 K0(3,5), *K2tog, K2tog tbl, K6(7,10),* rep from * to * twice more, K2tog, K2tog tbl, K0(4,5). *26(36,48) sts*

1ˢᵗ size only
Row 13 K2tog to end of row. *13 sts*
Row 14 P1, [P2tog] to end of row. *7 sts*
Cut yarn, thread through remaining sts and fasten off.

2ⁿᵈ and 3ʳᵈ sizes only.
Row 13 K(2,4), *K2tog, K2tog tbl, K(5,8),* repeat from * to * twice more, K2tog, K2tog tbl, K(3,4). *(28,40) sts*
Row 14 P.
Row 15 K(1,3), *K2tog, K2tog tbl, K(3,6),* repeat from * to * twice more, K2tog, K2tog tbl, K(2,3). *(20,32) sts*

3ʳᵈ size only
Row 17 K(2), *K2tog, K2tog tbl, K(4),* repeat from * to * twice more, K2tog, K2tog tbl, K(2). *(24) sts*

2ⁿᵈ and 3ʳᵈ sizes only
Next row P.
Next row [K2tog] to end of row. *(10,12) sts*
Next row [P2tog] to end of row. *(5,6) sts*
Cut yarn, thread through remaining sts and fasten off.

BOW
With 4mm (US 6) needles, cast on 5 sts.
Work in moss for 12.5cm/5in.
Cast off.

TO MAKE UP
Block and press work.
Join back seam.
Join the short sides of the bow together, wrap the centre with yarn and sew into place.

Plaits (make 2)
Cut 9 strands of contrast colour yarn in 90cm/18in lengths. Holding 3 of the strands together, thread this through one of the cast on edge stitches of the ear flap, pulling half the length through. Repeat this for the remaining 2 sets of 3 strands and work a plait to end, securing with a knot.

Long-sleeved Dress

With A Knitted Or Fabric Skirt

You will need

SIZE
1–2(2–3,3–4) years

Actual chest circumference:
56(61,66)cm/22(24,26)in

YARN
Rooster *Almerino DK*
For the bodice:
2(2,3) x 50g/1¾oz balls in main
colour *(Grape)*
1(1,1) x 50g/1¾oz balls in contrast
colour *(Lilac Sky)*

For the knitted skirt:
5(5,6) x 50g balls/1¾oz balls in
main colour

NEEDLES
Pair each of 3.75mm (US 5) and 4mm
(US 6) knitting needles.
3.75mm (US 5) circular needle
Stitch holder

TENSION
21 sts and 28 rows to 10cm/4in square
over st st using 4mm (US 6) needles

EXTRAS
For fabric skirt:
0.5(0.5,0.75)m/½(½,¾)yds of fabric,
and 0.5(0.75,0.75)m/½(¾,¾)yds of muslin for lining –
wash the muslin first to prevent future shrinkage.

Matching sewing thread

4 self-covered buttons (see page 120) or matching
buttons
Removable stitch markers or coloured yarn

10cm/4in square over st st using 4mm (US 6) needles

FRONT BODICE
With 4mm (US 6) needles, CC and using the thumb
method, cast on 61(67,73) sts.
K 2 rows.
Change to st st and work 5 rows.
Next row K. **
Change to MC and work straight in st st until front
measures 7(9,11)cm/2¾(3½,4¼)in from cast-on edge,
ending on a WS row.

Shape armholes
Cast off 4(4,5) sts at beg of next 2 rows. *53(59,63) sts*
Dec 1 st at each end of every row until
45(47,51) sts remain.
Dec 1 st at each end of next and every foll alt row until
39(41,45) sts remain.

Work straight until armhole measures 5(6,7)cm /2(2¼,2¾)in, ending on a WS row.

Shape neck
Left shoulder
Next row (RS) K14(14,16), turn and leave remaining 25(27,29) sts on a stitch holder.
Working on these 14(14,16) sts only, proceed thus:
Next row P.
Dec 1 st at neck edge on next 2 rows. *12(12,14) sts*
Dec 1 st at neck edge on next and every foll alt row until 9(9,11) sts remain.
Work straight until armhole measures 11(12,13)cm/4¼(4¾,5)in.
Cast off.

Right shoulder
With RS facing, and using the remaining 25(27,29) sts, leave the first 11(13,13) sts on the stitch holder (neck sts) and slip the rest onto the needle. *14(14,16) sts*
Re-join yarn and K to end.
Work as for left shoulder.

BACK BODICE
Work as for the front bodice to **.

Divide for back opening
Change to MC.
Next row (RS) K31(34,37), slip these sts onto a stitch holder, cast on 4 sts, K to end. *34(37,40) sts*

Left back
Next row P to last 5 sts, K5.
Next row K.
Rep last 2 rows until work measures 7(9,11)cm /2¾(3½,4¼)in from cast-on edge, ending on a RS row.

Shape armholes
Cast off 4(4,5) sts at beg of next row (armhole end). *30(33,35) sts*
Dec 1 st at armhole end of every row until 26(27,29) sts remain.
Dec 1 st at armhole end of next and every foll alt row until 23(24,26) sts remain.
Work straight until armhole measures 11(12,13)cm/ 4¼(4¾,5)in, ending on a WS row.
Cast off 14(15,15) sts at beg of next row (neck end), work to end.
Work 2 rows.

Cast off the remaining 9(9,11) sts.
With stitch markers or coloured yarn, mark even positions for 4 buttons along the garter st band.

Right back
With RS facing, slip the remaining 31(33,37) sts onto the needles.
K to the centre opening, cast on 3 sts. *34(36,40) sts*
Work as for left back, reversing the armhole shaping (the armhole cast off should be at beg of a RS row) and making a buttonhole to correspond with each of the button markers on the garter st band.

To make a buttonhole
With RS facing, K to the last 4 sts, K2tog, yf, k2.

SLEEVES (make 2)
Using 3.75 (US 5) needles and MC, cast on 33(35,37) sts.
K 2 rows.
Change to st st and work 8 rows.
Change to 4mm (US 6) needles
Cont in st st, inc 1 st at each end of 5ᵗʰ and every following 7ᵗʰ row until there are 43(47,53) sts.
Work straight until sleeve measures 17(20,24)cm /6¾(8,9½)in or required length, ending on a WS row.

Shape top
Cast off 4(4,5) sts at beg of next 2 rows. *35(39,43) sts*
Dec 1 st at each end of every row until 27(31,31) sts remain.
Dec 1 st at each end of next and every foll alt row until 19(19,23) sts remain.
Dec 1 st at each end of every row until 11 sts remain.
Cast off 2 sts at beg of next 2 rows.
Cast off remaining 7 sts.

BOW
For the dress with the knitted skirt
Bow
With 3.75 (US 5) needles and CC, cast on 11 sts.
K 54 rows.
Cast off.

Tails
With 3.75 (US 5) needles and CC, cast on 2 sts.
K 1 row.
Row 2 Inc into first st, K to end. *3 sts*
Row 3 K.
Rep last 2 rows until there are 11 sts.

K 40 rows.
Next row K2tog, K to end.
Next row K.
Rep last 2 rows until 2 sts remain.
K2tog and fasten off.

For the dress with the fabric skirt
Bow
With 3.75 (US 5) needles and CC, cast on 8 sts.
Every row Sl 1, K to end.
Work 36 rows.
Cast off.

KNITTED SKIRT

'Wrapping' a stitch
K required number of stitches, slip next stitch from left-hand needle to right-hand needle purlwise, keeping the yarn at the back of the work.
Bring yarn forward between the needles.
Slip stitch back onto the left-hand needle.
Turn your work. The yarn is now at the back of the work and the 'wrap' lies around the base of the slipped stitch. Continue as directed in pattern

Picking up the 'wrap'
Work up to the wrapped stitch and place the point of the right-hand needles up through the front of the wrap.
With the wrap on the needle, place the tip of the needle through the stitch it was wrapped around and knit the wrap and the stitch together

Using 4mm (US 6) needles and MC, cast on 66(78,92) sts.
Work 20(24,26) rows in st st, knitting 1 st at each end of every P row, ending on a WS row. **

Row 1 K to bottom edge.
Row 2 K61(73,87), wrap, turn.
Row 3 and every alt row K to the bottom edge unless otherwise stated.
Row 4 K56(68,82), wrap, turn.
Row 6 K51(63,77), wrap, turn.
Row 8 K46(58,72), wrap, turn.
Row 10 K41(53,67), wrap, turn.
Row 12 K36(48,62), wrap, turn.
Row 14 K31(43,57), wrap, turn.
Row 16 K26(38,52), wrap, turn.

Row 18 K21(33,47), wrap, turn.
Row 20 K16(28,42), wrap, turn.
Row 22 K11(23,37), wrap, turn.
Row 24 K6(18,32), wrap, turn.

2nd and 3rd sizes only
Row 26 K(13,27), wrap, turn.
Row 28 K(8,22), wrap, turn.
Row 30 K(3,17), wrap, turn.

3rd size only
Row 32 K(12), wrap, turn.
Row 34 K(7), wrap, turn.

All sizes
Row 1 K to the bottom edge.
Row 2 K to the top edge, picking up all the wrap sts on the way as described.
Row 3 and every alt row K to the bottom edge unless otherwise stated.
Row 4 K6(3,7), wrap, turn.
Row 6 K11(8,12) picking up the last wrap, wrap, turn.
Row 8 K16(13,17) picking up the last wrap, wrap, turn.
Row 10 K21(18,22) picking up the last wrap, wrap, turn.
Row 12 K26(23,27) picking up the last wrap, wrap, turn.
Row 14 K31(28,32) picking up the last wrap, wrap, turn.
Row 16 K36(33,37) picking up the last wrap, wrap, turn.
Row 18 K41(38,42) picking up the last wrap, wrap, turn.
Row 20 K46(43,47) picking up the last wrap, wrap, turn.
Row 22 K51(48,52) picking up the last wrap, wrap, turn.
Row 24 K56(53,57) picking up the last wrap, wrap, turn.
Row 26 K61(58,62) picking up the last wrap, wrap, turn.

2nd and 3rd sizes only
Row 28 K(63,67) picking up the last wrap, wrap, turn.
Row 30 K(68,72) picking up the last wrap, wrap, turn.

Row 32 K(73,77) picking up the last wrap, wrap, turn.

3rd size only
Row 34 K(82) picking up the last wrap, wrap, turn.
Row 36 K(87) picking up the last wrap, wrap, turn.

All sizes
Next row K to the bottom edge.
Next row K to the top edge, picking up the last wrap.
***
Work 40(48,52) rows in st st, knitting 1 st at each end of every P row, ending on a WS row. **
Rep from ** to ** twice more.
Rep from ** to *** once.
Work 20(24,26) rows in st st, knitting 1 st at each end of every P row, ending on a WS row.
Cast off.

Bottom edge
With 3.75mm (US 5) circular needle, RS facing and CC, pick up and K 360(440,490) sts evenly along the bottom edge.
Do not knit in the round, but go back and forth as if using straight needles.
Next row K.
Beg with a K row, work 7 rows in st st.
K 3 rows.
Change to MC and beg with a K row, work 5 rows in st st.
K 4 rows.
Cast off loosely.

TO MAKE UP
Both versions:
Block and press.
Join shoulder seams.
Fold the sleeves in half lengthways, place the fold to the shoulder seam and sew sleeves into place.
Join the sleeve and side seams.

Neck band
With RS facing, 3.75mm (US 5) needles, MC and beg at the button band, pick up and K into every st/row end up to the front stitch holder, K25(27,29) sts from stitch holder, pick up and K into every st/row end up to end of buttonhole band.
Cast off.

Knitted skirt
Join the centre back seam. Ease the skirt onto the bodice, joining with slip stitch so that bodice covers top skirt edge.

Fabric skirt
When making up the fabric skirt, remember to press at all stages.

1. For the skirt, cut a piece of fabric approx. 46(49,52)cm/18(19¼,20½)in long (adjust length as required) and 112cm/44in wide.

2. For the lining, cut a piece of pre-washed muslin 41(44,47)cm/16(17¼,18½)in long (adjust length as required; cut 5cm/2in shorted than fabric) and the same width as the main fabric.

TIP: for a fuller skirt increase the width of both the fabric and the lining.

3. With RSs together, sew the lining and the fabric together along one long edge.

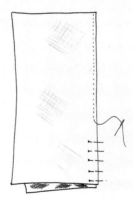

4. Join the second edges of the lining and the fabric.

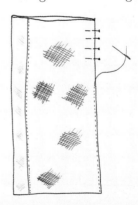

5. Press the seams toward the lining.

6. Turn the right way out, and press to form a hem at the bottom edge and no hem at the top (waist edge).

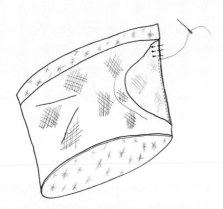

Pulling the lining out of the way and with RSs of the fabric together, join the centre back seam; join the main fabric first, then as much of the lining as possible.

7. Press the seam open.

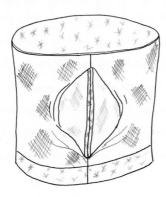

8. Turn the right way out, and using slip stitch close the gap in the lining.

9. Sew a line of gather stitches around the waist of the skirt.

10. With RS facing, pin and tack the bodice to the skirt, so that the bodice covers the gather stitches.

11. Turn to the inside and slip stitch the skirt into place. Stretch the bodice as you sew so that it is nice and stretchy.

Buttons
Cover the button (see page 120) and sew into place.

Bow
For the dress with the knitted skirt
With slip stitch join the short edges of the bow together and bind around the centre.
With a piece of matching yarn, sew into place on the left-hand side of the centre band.

For the dress with the fabric skirt
Follow the instructions for the knitted skirt, but without the tails.

Add fabric band along back neck if desired (see page 121).

Hampton

Hampton Court started life as a simple medieval manor in the fifteenth century. Over the years it has been rebuilt and altered and is very worthy of the title 'Palace'. It is a building steeped in Tudor History; it was the favourite home of Henry VIII and the birthplace of his son Edward in 1537.

The little mouse motif on the Hampton Court Collection was inspired by a visit to the Palace, when a small creature was spotted scurrying behind screens in the Great Hall.

Jumper

With Front Pocket

You will need

SIZE
1–2(3–4,5–6) years

Actual chest circumference:
61(65,69)cm/24(25½,27¼)in

YARN
Rowan *Pure Wool 4ply*
4(5,5) x 50g/1¾oz balls in main
colour *(Navy)*
1 x 50g/1¾oz ball in contrast colour
(Snow) for mouse
Scrap of pink for mouse nose

NEEDLES
3 x 3.25mm (US 3) knitting needles
Pair of 2.75 (US 2) knitting needles
Pair of 3.25mm (US 3) double-pointed
needles

TENSION
21 sts and 28 rows to 10cm/4in square
over st st using 4mm (US 6) needles

EXTRAS
Buttons: 3 x 15mm/½in buttons
Bead or button for mouse eye

BACK
With 3.25mm (US 3) needles and MC, cast on
87(93,99) sts.
Work 8 rows in moss st. **
Beg with a K row, work straight in st st until back
measures 23.5(28.5,36)cm/9¼(11¼,14¼)in, ending on a
WS row.

Shape armholes
Cast off 3 sts at beg of next 2 rows. *81(87,93) sts*
Dec 1 st at each end of next 3 rows. *75(81,87) sts*
Dec 1 st at each end of every RS row until 63(69,75) sts
remain. ***
Cont straight in st st until armhole measures
8(9,10)cm/3¼(3½,4)in, ending on a RS row.
Next row (WS) P31(34,37), K twice into next st,
P31(34,37). *64(70,76) sts*

Divide for back opening
Next row (RS) K32(35,38), slip these sts onto a stitch
holder, K to end.

Left back and shoulder
Next row (WS) Work to last 2 sts, K2, cast on 3 sts.
35(38,41) sts
Next row K.
Next row P to last 7 sts, K7.
Rep, last 2 rows until armhole measures 13(14,15)cm
/5(5½,6)in, ending on RS row.

Shape shoulder

Cast off 5(6,7) sts (shoulder edge) at beg of next row. *30(32,34) sts*

Work 1 row.

Cast off 5(6,7) sts (shoulder edge) at beg of next row. *25(26,27) sts*

Work 1 row.

Cast off 5(6,5) sts at beg of next row.

Leave remaining 20(20,22) sts on a stitch holder for the neck band.

With stitch markers or coloured yarn, mark 2 button places evenly on the garter st edge.

Right back and shoulder

Slip the 32(35,38) right side sts onto the needle.

With RS facing, re-join yarn at armhole edge, K to end, cast on 3 sts. *35(38,41) sts*

Next row K7, P to end.

Next row K.

Rep last 2 rows until armhole measures 13(14,15)cm/ 5(5½,6)in, ending on a RS row.

AT THE SAME TIME, make 2 buttonholes to correspond with the button markings thus:

With WS facing, K3, yf, K2tog, K2, P to end of row.

Shape shoulder

Cast off 5(6,7) sts (shoulder edge) at beg of next row. *30(32,34) sts*

Work 1 row.

Cast off 5(6,7) sts (shoulder edge) at beg of next row. *25(26,27) sts*

Work 1 row.

Cast off 5(6,5) sts at beg of next row.

Leave remaining 20(20,22) sts on a stitch holder.

FRONT

Work as for back to **.

Beg with a K row, work straight in st st until front measures 10(10,11)cm/4(4,4¼)in, ending on a WS row.

Divide for pocket

Next row (RS) K29(31,33), K the following 29(31,33) sts and slip these centre sts onto a stitch holder for the pocket, K29(31,33).

Next row P29(31,33), cast on 29(31,33), P29(31,33). *87(93,99) sts*

Next row K.

Next row P20(23,26), join in CC and using the intarsia method begin working the mouse motif from row 2 of the chart (48 sts), P19(22,25).

Cont working the mouse chart right up to row 30 (ending on a WS row).

Slip the pocket sts from the stitch holder onto the spare 3.25mm (US 3) needle and with WS facing, work these 29(31,33) sts in st st for 31 rows (ending on a WS row).

Re-join pocket

Next row (RS) K29(31,33), then take a st from the body and a stitch from the pocket and K the two together, do this until all the pocket sts are used, K29(31,33). *87(93,99) sts*

Cont as for back to ***.

Work straight until armhole measures 9(9,9.5)cm/ 3½(3½,3¾), ending on a WS row.

Divide for front neck

Next row (RS) K23(26,29), turn and work on these sts only (leaving rem 40(43,46) sts on a stitch holder).

Left shoulder

Dec 1 st at neck edge of next 4 rows. *19(22,25) sts*

Dec 1 st at neck edge of foll 4(5,6) RS rows. *15(17,19) sts*

Work 1 row.

Shape shoulder

Cast off 5(6,7) sts at beg of next and foll alt row (armhole edge).

Work 1 row.

Cast off the remaining 5 sts.

Right shoulder

Slip the centre 17 sts onto another stitch holder and the rem 23(26,29) sts onto the needle so that the RS is facing.

Re-join yarn and K 1 row.

Dec 1 st at neck edge of next 4 rows.

Dec 1 st at neck edge of foll 4(5,6) RS rows. *15(17,19) sts*

Work 2 rows.

Shape shoulder

Cast off 5(6,7) sts at beg of next and foll alt row (armhole edge).

Work 1 row.

Cast off the remaining 5 sts.

SLEEVES

Using 2.75mm (US 2) needles and MC, cast on 43(45,47) sts.

Work 10 rows in moss st.

Change to 3.25mm (US 3) needles and beg with a K row, work in st st throughout.

Inc 1 st at each end of 3rd and every foll 5th row until there are 73(79,85) sts.

Cont straight until sleeve measures 23(27,30)cm/9(10¾,11¾)in or required length, ending on a WS row.

Shape top

Cast off 3 st at beg of next 2 rows. *67(73,79) sts*

Dec 1 st at each end of next 5 rows. *57(63,69) sts*

Dec 1 st at each end of next 5 RS rows. *47(53,59) sts*

Dec 1 st at each end of every row until 17(19,21) sts remain, ending on a WS row.

Cast off.

MOUSE EAR

Using 3.25mm (US 3) needles and CC, cast on 7 sts.

Beg with a K row, work 4 rows in st st.

Row 5 K2tog, K to last 2 sts, K2tog. *5 sts*

Row 6 P2tog, P to last 2 sts, P2tog. *3 sts*

Row 7 P.

Cast off rem 3 sts.

MOUSE TAIL

With 3.25mm (US 3) double-pointed needles and CC, cast on 4 sts and make an I-cord:

K to end of row.

*Slide the sts to the right-hand side of the needle.

Pull yarn taut and K another row. *

Rep from * to * until the I-cord is 28cm/11in long.

Cut yarn, thread through the sts and fasten off.

TO MAKE UP

Block and press work.

Using mattress st, join both shoulder seams.

Neck band

With 2.75mm (US 2) needles, MC and RS facing, beg at the back opening, K20(20,22) sts from the left back stitch holder, pick up and K17(18,20) sts down the left side front neck, K17 from the front stitch holder, pick up and K17(18,20) sts up the right side front neck, K20(20,22) from the right back holder. *91(93,101) sts*

Next row (WS) K3, yf, K2tog, K to end of row.

K 4 rows.

Cast off.

Fold the sleeves in two lengthways, marry the fold line with the shoulder seam and sew the sleeve into place.

Sew the sleeve and side seams.

Sew a small row of backs sts to define the mouse's back leg.

Sew a bead/button (or in the case of very small children make a French knot for the eye (see page 122)).

With a scrap of pink yarn, french knot a small nose.

Sew the ear into place.

Sew tail into place and arrange as required.

Pocket welts

With RS facing and beg at the top of the pocket on the right-hand side and the bottom of the pocket on the left-hand side, pick up and K 22 sts evenly along the edge.

Cast off.

Overlap the buttonhole band over the button band and sew into place at the bottom.

Sew on buttons to correspond with buttonholes.

CHART

RS: Knit
WS: Purl

Main colour

Contrast colour

Position of eye

Position of legs

Position of ears

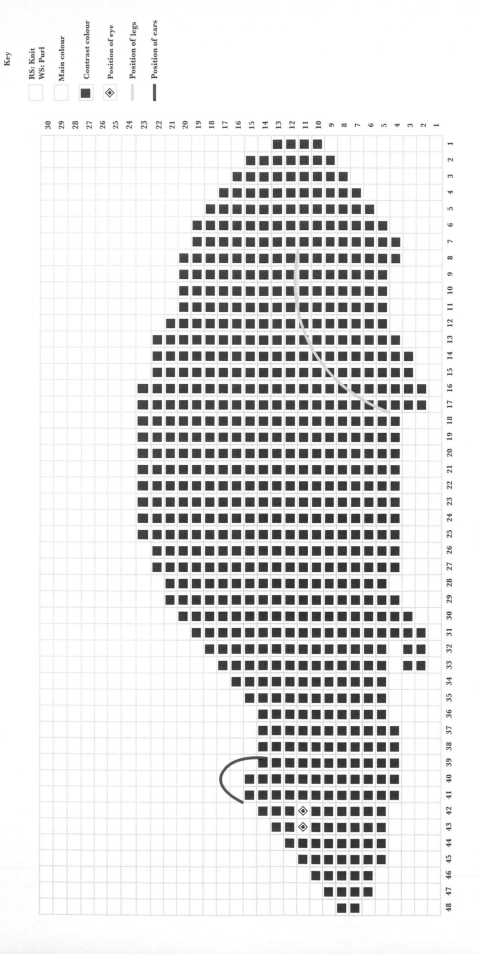

Hat

With Mouse Detail

HAT

With 3.25mm (US 3) needles and MC, cast on
102(110,118) sts.
Row 1 K2, [P2, K2] to end.
Row 2 P2, [K2, P2] to end.
Rep last 2 rows (in K2, P2 rib) until work measures
4(5,6)cm/1½(2,2¼)in, ending on a WS row.
Beg with K row, work 10 rows in st st.
Next row K34(36,40), join in CC and using the intarsia
method, work Row 1 of the mouse motif, K to end.
Cont in this way until the 19 rows of the chart have been
worked.
With MC, work another 11(15,17) rows straight, ending
on a WS row.

Shape top
Row 1 (RS) *K2, K2tog tbl, K19(21,23), K2tog*, rep
from * to * to last 2 sts, K2. *94(102,110) sts*
Row 2 and every alt row P.
Row 3 *K2, K2tog tbl, K17(19,21), K2tog*, rep from * to
* to last 2 sts, K2. *86(94,102) sts*
Row 5 *K2, K2tog tbl, K15(17,19), K2tog*, rep from * to
* to last 2 sts, K2. *78(86,94) sts*
Row 7 *K2, K2tog tbl, K13(15,17), K2tog*, rep from * to
* to last 2 sts, K2. *70(78,86) sts*
Row 9 *K2, K2tog tbl, K11(13,15), K2tog*, rep from * to
* to last 2 sts, K2. *62(70,78) sts*
Row 11 *K2, K2tog tbl, K9(11,13), K2tog*, rep from *
to * to last 2 sts, K2. *54(62,70) sts*
Row 13 *K2, K2tog tbl, K7(9,11), K2tog*, rep from * to
* to last 2 sts, K2. *46(54,62) sts*

Row 15 *K2, K2tog tbl, K5(7,9), K2tog*, rep from * to * to last 2 sts, K2. *38(46,54) sts*
Row 17 *K2, K2tog tbl, K3(5,7), K2tog*, rep from * to * to last 2 sts, K2. *30(38,46) sts*
Row 19 *K2, K2tog tbl, K1(3,5), K2tog*, rep from * to * to last 2 sts, K2. *22(30,38) sts*

2nd and 3rd size only
Row 21 *K2, K2tog tbl, K(1,3), K2tog*, rep from * to * to last 2 sts, K2. *(22,30) sts*

3rd size only
Row 23 *K2, K2tog tbl, K(1), K2tog*, rep from * to * to last 2 sts, K2. *(22) sts*

All sizes
Next row (WS) P.
Next row *K1, K2tog tbl, K2tog*, rep from * to * to last 2 sts, K2. *14 sts*
Work 15 rows straight in st st.
Thread yarn through rem sts and fasten off, leaving a long end to sew the back seam.

EAR
With 3.25mm (US 3) needles and CC, cast on 3 sts.
Row 1 K.
Row 2 P.
Next row K2tog, slip last st back onto the left-hand needle, K2tog tbl.
Fasten off.

TAIL
With 2.75mm (US 2) double-pointed needles and CC, cast on 2 sts and work an I-cord thus:
K to end of row
*Slide the sts to the right-hand side of the needle.
Pull yarn taut and K another row*
Rep from * to * until the 'tail' is 12cm/4¾in long.
Next row K2tog and fasten off.

TO MAKE UP
Block and press work.
Sew the back seam.
Sew the ear into place.
Sew a bead or form a French knot (see page 120) for the eye.
Sew the tail into place and arrange as required.
Sew a pink French knot (see page 120) for the nose.

CHART

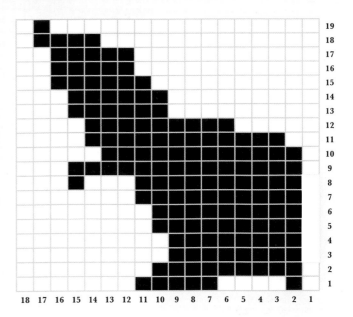

18 17 16 15 14 13 12 11 10 9 8 7 6 5 4 3 2 1

Key

☐ **RS: Knit**
  WS: Purl

☐ **Main colour**

■ **Contrast colour**

Cardigan

With Mouse Detail

You will need

SIZE
1–2(3–4,5–6) years

Actual chest circumference:
62(68,73)cm/24½(26¾,28¾)in

YARN
Rowan *Pure Wool 4ply*
3(4,4) x 50g/1¾oz balls in main colour *(Navy)*
1 x 50g/1¾oz ball in contrast colour *(Snow)*
for mouse
Scrap of pink for mouse nose

NEEDLES
Pair each of 2.75mm (US 2) and 3.25mm
(US 3) knitting needles
Pair of 2.75mm (US 2) double-pointed
needles for the tail

EXTRAS
9(9,10) x 15mm/½in buttons

TENSION
28 sts and 36 rows to 10cm/4in square
over st st using 3.25mm (US 3) needles

BACK
With 3.25mm (US 3) needles and MC, cast on
87(95,103) sts.
Work 10 rows in moss st.
Beg with a K row, work straight in st st until back
measures 23(26,31)cm/9(10¼,12¼)in, ending on a
WS row.

Shape raglan
Cast off 5 sts at beg of next 2 rows. *77(85,93) sts*
Dec 1 st at each end of every row until
65(69,69) sts remain.
Dec 1 st at each end of next and every foll alt row until
29(33,33) sts remain.
Slip remaining sts onto a stitch holder.

RIGHT FRONT
With 3.25mm (US 3) needles and MC, cast on
45(50,54) sts.
Work 10 rows in moss st.
Beg with a K row, work 4 rows in st st.
Next row (RS) Work 8(10,12) sts, join in CC and using
the intarsia method, work the 28 sts of the chart, work to
end of row.
Cont working the chart until all 43 rows have
been worked.
Work straight in MC only until front measures 23(26,31)
cm /9(10¼,12¼)in, ending on a RS row.

Shape raglan

Cast off 5 sts at beg of next row. *40(45,49) sts*
Dec 1 st at raglan edge on every row until 31(33,33) sts remain.
Dec 1 st at raglan edge on next and every foll alt row until 19(21,21) sts remain, ending on a WS row.

Shape neck

Cast off 6(7,7) sts at beg (neck edge) of next row. *13(14,14) sts*
Work 5(6,6) rows dec 1 st at raglan edge on the next and every foll alt row, AND AT THE SAME TIME, dec 1 st at neck edge on every row. *5 sts*
Work 6(5,5) rows dec 1 st at raglan edge only on 2nd(1st,1st) and every foll alt row. *2 sts*
Next row K2tog and fasten off.

LEFT FRONT

With 3.25 mm (US 3) needles and MC, cast on 45(50,54) sts.
Work 10 rows in moss st.
Beg with a K row, work 4 rows in st st.
Work straight in st st until front measures 23(26,31)cm /9(10¼,12¼)in, ending on a WS row.

Shape raglan

Cast off 5 sts at beg of next row. *40(45,49) sts*
P 1 row.
Dec 1 st at raglan edge on every row until 31(33,33) sts remain.
Dec 1 st at raglan edge on next and every foll alt row until 20(22,22) sts remain, ending on a RS row.

Shape neck

Next row Cast off 6(7,7) sts at neck edge, work to last 2 sts, P2tog. *13(14,14) sts*
Next row K.
Work 5(6,6) rows dec 1 st at neck edge on every row, AND AT THE SAME TIME, dec 1 st at raglan on edge on next and every foll alt row. *5 sts*
Work 6(5,5) rows dec 1 st at raglan edge only on 2nd(1st,1st) and every foll alt row. *2 sts*
Next row P2tog and fasten off.

SLEEVES (make 2)

With 2.75mm (US 2) needles and MC, cast on 51(57,59) sts.
Row 1 K1, [P1, K1] to end.
Row 2 P1, [K1, P1] to end.

Rep Rows 1 & 2 (K1, P1 rib) until work measures 3cm/1¼in.
Change to 3.25mm (US 3) needles
Beg with a K row, work 4 rows in st st.
Inc 1 st at each end of next and every foll 4th(5th,5th) row until there are 65(67,77) sts.
Inc 1 st at each end of every foll 10th(12th,12th) row until there are 67(73,79) sts.
Cont straight until sleeve measures 24(29,33)cm/ 9½(11½,13)in or required length, ending on a WS row.

Shape raglan

Cast off 5 sts at beg of next 2 rows. *57(63,69) sts*
Dec 1 st at each end of every row until 55(59,61) sts remain.
Dec 1 st at each end of next and every foll alt row until 17 sts remain.
Slip remaining sts onto a stitch holder.

POCKET

Using 3.25mm (US 3) needles and MC, cast on 28 sts.
K 2 rows. (This will be the bottom edge of the pocket.)
Beg with a K row, work in st st until the pocket measures 7.5cm/3in.
Change to moss st and work another 3cm/1¼in.
Cast off.

MOUSE EAR

Using 3.25mm (US 3) needles and CC, cast on 7 sts.
Beg with a K row, work 4 rows in st st.
Row 5 K2tog, K to last 2 sts, K2tog. *5 sts*
Row 6 P2tog, P to last 2 sts, P2tog. *3 sts*
Row 7 P.
Cast off rem 3 sts.

MOUSE TAIL

With 2.75mm (US 2) double-pointed needles and CC, cast on 4 sts and make an I-cord:
K to end of row.
*Slide the sts to the right-hand side of the needle.
Pull yarn taut and K another row. *
Rep from * to * until the I-cord is 28cm/11in long.
Cut yarn, thread through the sts and fasten off.

TO MAKE UP

Neck band

Block and press work.
Join raglan seams.

With 2.75mm (US 2) needles, MC and RS facing, and beg at right front, pick up and K17(18,18) sts from side of neck, K17 from sleeve stitch holder, K29(33,33) sts from back stitch holder, K17 from second sleeve stitch holder, pick up and K 17(18,18) sts from side of left neck. *97(104,104) sts*
Work 6 rows in moss st.
Cast off.

Right front border

With 2.75mm (US 2) needles, MC and RS facing, and beg at the bottom edge, pick up and K 97(111,129) sts evenly from front border and 5 sts from neck band.
Work 9 rows in moss st.
Cast off.
With stitch markers or coloured yarn, evenly mark 9(9,10) positions for the buttons.

Left front border

With 2.75mm (US 2) needles, MC and RS facing, and beg at the top edge, pick up and 5 sts from neck band and K 97(111,129) sts evenly from front border.
Work 4 rows in moss st.
Next row Make a buttonhole to correspond with each of the button markers (to make a buttonhole, yf, K2tog).
Work 4 rows in moss st.
Cast off.

To finish the mouse motif

Split a length of the main yarn into 4 strands and, using 1 strand and stem st (see page 123), sew a line of stitches to define the limbs.
Sew the ear into place.
Sew a bead or a French knot (see page 122) for the eye.
Sew a pink French knot for the nose.
Split a length of white yarn into 4 strands and, using 1 strand, sew whiskers on the side of the nose.
Sew tail into position.
Turn the moss st border over to the right side of the pocket and sew into place.
Sew the pocket into place so that the top third of the mouse is visible and the tail hangs over the top of the pocket.
Join the sleeve and side seams.
Sew the buttons to correspond with the buttonholes.

CHART

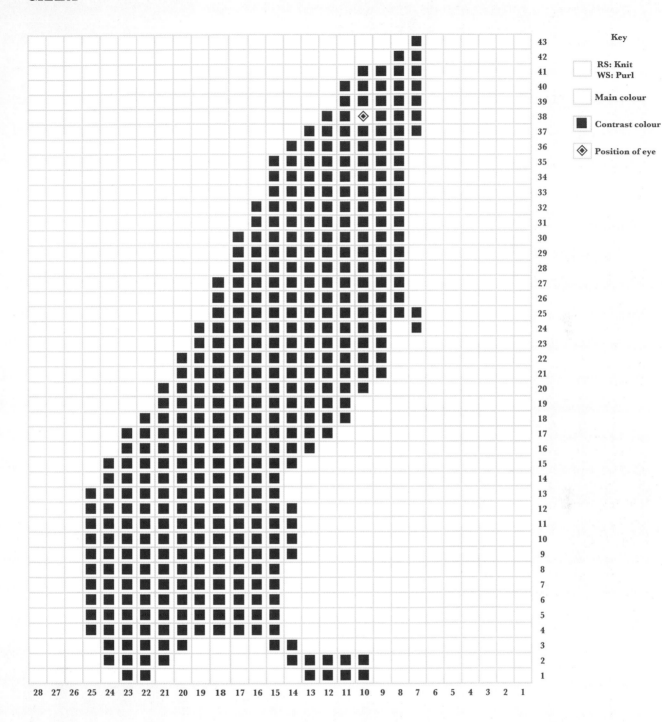

Mouse Scarf

You will need

SIZE
One size – child 1–6 years

YARN
Rowan *Pure Wool 4 ply*
3 x 50g/1¾oz balls in main colour *(Snow)*
1 x 50g/1¾oz ball in pale pink for mouth
scraps of grey for nose

NEEDLES
Pair each of 3mm (US 2/3) and 4.5mm
(US 7) knitting needles
Pair each of 3mm (US 2/3), 3.5mm
(US 4) and 4mm (US 6) double-pointed
needles

EXTRAS
2 buttons, beads or safety eyes (for very
small children work eyes and nose in
coloured yarn)

TENSION
28 sts and 36 rows to 10cm/4in square 20
sts and 37 rows to 10cm/4in square over
garter st with 4.5mm (US 7) needles and
yarn held double

WARNING
Never leave a young child alone wearing a scarf.

SCARF
Work with 2 strands and in garter st, throughout.
Using 4.5mm (US 7) needles and 2 strands of MC, cast on
4 sts.
Row 1 M2 into first st, K1, M2 into next st, K1. *8 sts*
K 3 rows.
Row 5 K1, M2 into next st, K3, M2 into next st, K2.
12 sts
K 3 rows.
Row 9 K2, M2 into next st, K5, M2 into next st, K3.
16 sts
K 3 rows.
Row 13 K3 inc twice into next st K7, inc twice into next
st K4. *20 sts*
K 3 rows.
Cont in this way, inc 4 sts on next and every foll 4th row
until there are 44 sts.
Next row K2tog, K to last 2 sts, K2tog. *42 sts.*
Rep last row until 22 sts remain.
Work straight until scarf measures 86cm/34in or
required length.
Cast off 2 sts at beg of each row until 6 sts remain.
Slip these 6 sts onto 4mm (US 6) double-pointed needles
and work an I-cord.

To make an I-cord
K to end of row.
*Slide the sts to the right-hand side of the needle.

Pull yarn taut and K another row. *
Rep from * to * until the 'tail' is 18cm/7in long.
Change to 3.5mm (US 4) double-pointed needles
and work I-cord for another 4cm/1½in.
Change to 3mm (US 2/3) double-pointed needles
and work I-cord until the tail measures 32cm/12½in
or required length. P6tog.
Fasten off.

LOWER JAW

With 4.5mm (US 7) needles and 2 strands of MC, cast
on 4 sts.
Working in garter st, inc 1 st at each end of every 4th
row until there are 22sts.
K 11 rows straight.
Cast off.

MOUTH

With 4.5mm (US 7) needles and 2 strands of pink
yarn, cast on 4 sts.
Working in garter st, inc 1 st at each end of every 4th
row until there are 12 sts.
Next row P.
Next row K.
Next row P.
Working in garter st, dec 1 st at each end of next and
every 4th row until 4 sts remain.
K 3 rows.
Cast off.

OUTER EARS (make 2)

With 4.5mm (US 7) needles and 2 strands of main
yarn cast on 5 sts.
Row 1 K1, M1 into next 2 sts, K2. *7 sts*
Row 2 P2, M1 into next 2 sts, P3. *9 sts*
Row 3 M1 into first st, K6, M1 into next st, K1. *11 sts*
Row 4 M1 into first st, P8, M1 into next st, P1. *13 sts*
Row 5 K1, [M1 into next st, K2] to end of row. *17 sts*
Work 7 rows in st st.
Row 13 [Skpo] twice, K9, [K2tog] twice. *13 sts*
Row 14 P.
Row 15 Skpo, K7, K2tog K2. *11 sts*
Row 16 P.
Row 17 Skpo, K1, K3tog, K1, K2tog, K2. *7 sts*
Row 18 P.
Row 19 Skpo, K3, K2tog. *5 sts*
Row 20 P.
Cast off.

INNER EARS (make 2)

With 3.25mm (US 3) needles and 1 strand of pink
yarn, cast on 5 sts.
Row 1 K1, M1 into next 2 sts, K2. *7 sts*
Row 2 P2, M1 into next st, P3. *9 sts*
Row 3 M1 into first st, K6, M1 into next st, K1. *11 sts*
Row 4 M1 into first st, P8, M1 into next st, P1. *13 sts*
Row 5 K1, [M1 into next st, K2] to end of row. *17 sts*
Row 6 P1, [M1 into next st, P2] to last st. P1. *22 sts*
Work 8 rows in st st.
Row 15 [Skpo] twice, K14, [K2tog] twice. *18 sts*
Row 16 P.
Row 17 [Skpo] twice, K10, [K2tog] twice. *14 sts*
Row 18 P.
Row 19 Sk2po, K7, [K2tog] twice. *10 sts*
Row 20 P.
Row 21 Skpo, K6, K2tog. *8 sts*
Row 22 P.
Row 23 Skpo, K4, K2tog. *6 sts*
Row 24 P.
Cast off.

TO MAKE UP

Fold the mouth in two and, using mattress st, sew the
top half to the nose end of the main piece.
Sew the bottom half to the lower jaw.
Using mattress st, sew the sides of the bottom jaw to
the sides of the head.
Using mattress st, sew the inner and the outer ears
together and sew the ears into place.
Sew beads/buttons into place for eyes, or use black
yarn and French knots (see page 122).
With grey yarn and satin stitch, sew the nose.
Sew whiskers into place each side of nose by using
yarn and knotting it each side of the face.
Using mattress st, sew the tail decrease together so
that it tapers into the tail.

Mouse Rucksack

NOTE
Work 3 strands of yarn unless otherwise stated

BODY OF RUCKSACK
Knitted in one beginning at the flap.
With 5.5mm (US 9) needles and 3 strands of MC, cast on
26 sts.

Flap
K 5 rows.
Row 6 K4, cast off 3sts, K to last 7 sts, cast off 3 sts,
K to end.
Row 7, cast on 3 sts, K to last 4 sts, cast on 3 sts,
K to end.
Row 8 Inc into first st, K to last 2 sts, inc into next st, K1.
28 sts
Row 9 As Row 7. *30 sts*
Row 10 Inc into first st, K5, P to last 6 sts, K4, inc into
next st, K1. *32 sts*
Row 11 Inc into first st, K to last 2 sts, inc into next st,
K1. *34 sts*

Row 12 K8, P to last 8 sts, K8.
Row 13 K.
Rep last 2 rows 7 times more.
K 6 rows.

Back
Next row (WS) Cast on 6 sts, P to end. *40 sts*
Next row Cast on 6 sts, K to end. *46 sts*
Next row K6, P to last 6 sts, K6.
Next row K.
Rep last 2 rows 31 times more.
Cast off 6 sts at beg of next 2 rows. *34 sts*
K 7 rows.

Front
Beg with a K row, work 2 rows in st st.
Join in CC and using the intarsia method, work the
43 rows of the chart.
Work 13 rows in st st.
K 3 rows.
Next row K3, *yf, K2tog, K3* rep from * to * to last
st, K1.
K 4 rows.
Cast off.

MOUSE TAIL
With 4mm (US 6) double-pointed needles and 1
strand of DK in contrast colour, cast on 4 sts and
make an I-cord:
K to end of row.
*Slide the sts to the right-hand side of the needle.
Pull yarn taut and K another row. *
Rep from * to * until the I-cord is 30cm/12in long.
Cut yarn, thread through the sts and fasten off.

MAKE AN I-CORD FOR TOP OF FRONT
With 3.25mm (US 3) double-pointed needles and
1 strand of MC, work as for tail until the I-cord is
60cm/24in long.
Do not sew the ends of the yarn in as they will be
used for threading the toggle button.

STRAPS (make 2)
With 5.5mm (US 9) needles and 2 strands of MC, cast
on 12 sts.
Work in st st until strap measures 35cm/14in for a
small child or up to approx. 50cm/20in for a
bigger child.
Cast off.

ANCHORS (make 2)
With 5.5mm (US 9) needles and 2 strands of MC, cast
on 6 sts.
K 12 rows.
Cast off.

POCKET
Using 5.5 mm (US 9) needles and 3 strands of MC,
cast on 28 sts.
K 4 rows.
Next row K.
Next row K6, P to last 6 sts, K6.
Rep last 2 rows 8 times more.
K 4 rows.
Cast off.

MOUSE EAR
Using 5.5mm (US 9) needles and 2 strands of MC,
cast on 6 sts.
Row 1 K2, M1 into next st, K to end. *7 sts*
Row 2 K1, P to last st, K1.
Row 3 K3, M1 into next st, K to end. *8 sts*
Row 4 K1, P to last st, K1.
Row 5 K2tog, K1, K2tog, K1, K2tog. *5 sts*
Row 6 P2tog, P1, P2tog. *3 sts*
Row 7 K1, P1, K1.
Row 8 P.
Row 9 K2tog, K1. *2 sts*
Row 10 Skpo.
Fasten off.

TO MAKE UP
Block and press work.
Using stem st (see page 123) define the mouse's legs
as indicated on the chart (see page 51).
Sew the ear to the head and sew a bead or button to
indicate the eye (with very small children use a large
French knot (see page 122)).
Sew the nose with pink yarn.
Sew several single strands of yarn into place from
the nose to indicate whiskers.
Sew the pocket into place so that the mouse is
showing above the pocket, as in the photograph.

If the rucksack is to be lined, lay the work onto a piece of paper and, excluding the flap, draw around the edge. Draw around the edge again to indicate a 2cm/¾in ease and seam allowance.

Place and pin the pattern onto the fabric and cut out.

To make up the lining:
Pin point A to point B and point C to point D.

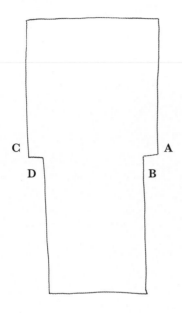

Sew the gusset into place.

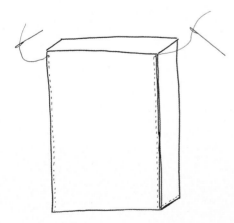

Sew tail onto the mouse so that it hangs over the top of the pocket.

For the top cord: Thread the cast-on and cast-off ends onto a needle and pass them both together through the toggle button so the cord forms a loop. Slide the toggle button to within approx. 5cm/2in of the centre of the loop. Beg at the centre, thread the cord either way through the holes at the top of the front and secure each side.

Using mattress st, sew the gusset into place as for the lining.

Thread clips through anchor straps, fold in two and sew to bottom edges of back section.

Fold the straps in two lengthways, wrap around the tape leaving a long end (clip end). Sew the tape and the strap together securely at the top end.

Using slip st, oversew the strap around the tape, being sure not to catch the tape in the strap.

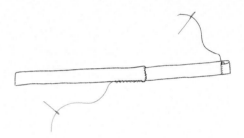

Stretch the strap slightly and sew the clip end of the strap to the tape, leaving the long end of the tape free. Thread this end of the tape through the rucksack clip. Securely sew the straps onto the back of the rucksack approx. 2cm/¾in in from the gusset as shown in diagram.

Thread the anchor straps through the other end of the rucksack clip and sew into place at the bottom corners of the rucksack.

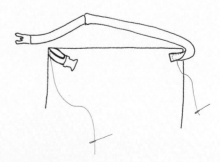

Sew buttons to correspond with buttonholes.

CHART

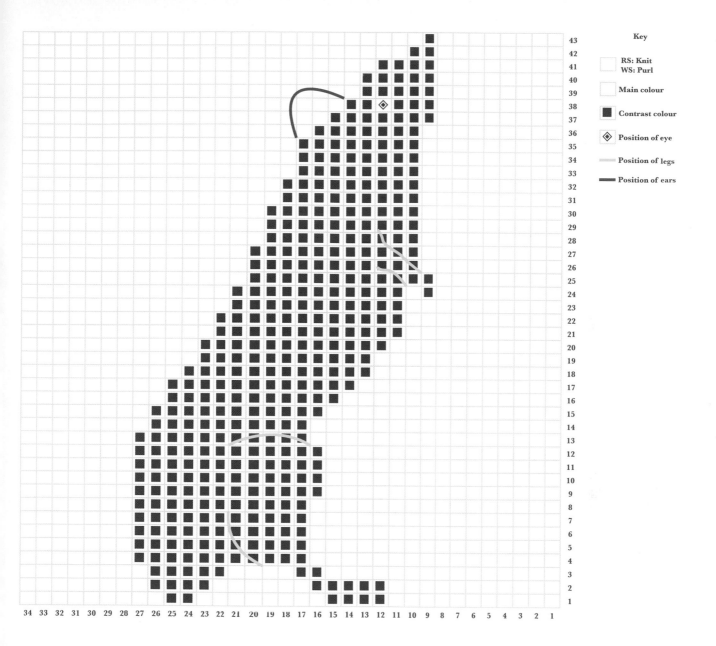

Key

RS: Knit
WS: Purl

Main colour

Contrast colour

Position of eye

Position of legs

Position of ears

51

Kensington K

Kensington Palace, once home to the Royal Court, is now the home to many Royals including Prince Harry, the Duke and Duchess of Kent and the Duke and Duchess of Gloucester, and is the London home to the Duke and Duchess of Cambridge and their two children, Prince George and Princess Charlotte. It was once described by Andrew Morton as being a 'children's paradise' with its long passageways, a helicopter pad and many outdoor gardens, including one on the roof where the late Princess Diana and her children spent many happy hours.

The Kensington Palace Collection is designed to echo happy childhood memories, with the soft colours and pretty prints, it has an air of carefree living and childhood laughter.

Butterfly Jumper

You will need

SIZE
1–2(2–3,3–4) years

Actual chest circumference: 59(64,69)cm /23¼(25¼,27¼)in

YARN
Rooster *Baby Rooster*
4(5,5) x 50g/1¾oz balls in main colour *(Vintage Rose)*
1 x 50g/1¾oz ball for butterfly in contrast colour *(Parma Violet)*

NEEDLES
Pair each of 3mm (US 2/3) and 3.25mm (US 3) knitting needles
Set each of 3mm (US 2/3) and 3.25mm (US 3) double-pointed needles for the neck
Stitch holders

TENSION
25 sts and 34 rows to 10cm/4in square over st st using 3.25mm (US 3) needles

BACK
With 3mm (US 2/3) needles and MC, cast on 74(80,86) sts.
Row 1 P2, [K4, P2] to end.
Row 2 P.
Rep last 2 rows 8 times more. **
Change to 3.25mm (US 3) needles and beg with a K row, work in st st until back measures 23(23.5,24)cm/9(9¼,9½) in from cast-on edge, ending on a WS row.

Shape armholes
Cast off 4 sts at beg of next 2 rows. *66(72,78) sts*
Next row (RS) K2, K2tog tbl, K to last 4 sts, K2tog, K2. *64(70,76) sts*
Next row P.
Rep last 2 rows 3(4,5) times more. *58(62,66) sts*
Cont straight until back measures 37(37.5,38)cm /14½(14¾,15)in, ending on a WS row.

Shape shoulders
Cast off 14(15,16) sts at beg of next 2 rows.
Leave the remaining 30(32,34) sts on stitch holder.

FRONT
Work as for back to **
Change to 3.25mm (US 3) needles and beg with a K row, work in st st until front measures 12(14,15)cm/ 4¾(5½,6)in from cast-on edge, ending on a WS row.
Next row (RS) K11(14,17), join in CC and using intarsia method beg working the butterfly chart (52 sts), K11(14,17).

Cont straight, working the butterfly chart in the centre of the front, until front measures 23(23.5,24)cm /9(9¼,9½)in from cast-on edge, ending on a WS row.

Shape armholes

Cast off 4 sts at beg of next 2 rows. *66(72,78) sts*

Next row (RS) K2, K2tog tbl, K to last 4 sts K2tog, K2. *64(70,76) sts*

Next row P.

Rep last 2 rows 3(4,5) times more. *58(62,66) sts*

Cont straight until front measures 31(31.5,32)cm /12¼(12½,12¾)in, ending on a WS row.

Divide for neck and shoulders
Left shoulder

Row 1 K18(19,20), turn and leave rem sts on a stitch holder.

Working on these 18(19,20) sts only, proceed thus:

Next row (WS) P.

Next row K to last 4 sts, K2tog, K2. *17(18,19) sts*

Rep last 2 rows 3 times more. *14(15,16) sts*

Cont straight until front measures the same as back. Cast off.

Right shoulder

With RS facing, leave first 22(24,26) sts (neck sts) on a stitch holder, re-join yarn at neck edge, K to end. *18(19,20) sts*

Next row (WS) P.

Next row K2, K2tog tbl, K to end. *17(18,19) sts*

Rep last 2 rows 3 times more. *14(15,16) sts.*

Cont straight until front measures the same as back. Cast off.

SLEEVES

With 3mm (US 2/3) needles and MC, cast on 32(38,44) sts.

Row 1 P2, [K4, P2] to end.

Row 2 K2, [P4, K2] to end.

Rep these 2 rows 6(7,7) times more.

Change to 3.25mm (US 3) needles.

Beg with a K row, work 2 rows in st st.

* Inc row (RS) K3, M1, K to last 3 sts, M1, K3. *34(40,46) sts*

Work 5 rows in st st. *

Rep from * to * 6(7,8) times more, then Inc row once more. *48(56,64) sts*

Cont straight until sleeve measures 19(22,24)cm /7½(8¾,9½)in or required length from cast-on edge, ending on the WS.

Shape top

Cast off 4 sts at beg of next 2 rows. *40(48,56) sts*

Next row (RS) K2, K2tog tbl, K to last 4 sts, K2tog, K2. *38(46,54) sts*

Next row P.

Rep last 2 rows 11(13,15) times more. *16(20,24) sts*

Cast off 2 sts at beg of next 4 rows.

Cast off rem 8(12,16) sts.

TO MAKE UP

If you wish to work the neckband straight (on 2 needles), join just one shoulder seam and work the neck band as directed below, working it back and forth in st st and joining it at the same time as the shoulder seam.

Block and press work.
Join the shoulder seams.

Shoulder frill (both alike)
With 3mm (US 2/3) needles, RS facing and beg and ending at the top of the armhole shaping, pick up and K42(44,46) sts around the armhole.
Row 2 P.
Row 3 M1 into every st. *84(88,92) sts*
Row 4 P.
Row 5 M1 into every st. *168(176,184) sts*
Row 6 P.
Cast off loosely.
Press the very edge of the frills.

Using slip st, sew the little side edge at each end of the frill to the armhole edge so that the frill tapers. Fold the frill to the RS of the work and pin or tack into position to hold it away from the armhole edge whilst sewing in the sleeve.
Mark the centre of the sleeve top.
Using mattress st, sew the sleeve into position.
Remove the pins or tacking sts.
Finger press the frill outwards toward the sleeve.
Join sleeve and side seams.

Neck roll
With 3mm (US 2/3) double-pointed needles, RS facing, MC and beg at the left shoulder, pick up and K12(15,18) sts from the left front neck, K22(24,26) sts from the front stitch holder, pick up and K12(15,18) sts from the right front neck, K30(32,34) sts from the back stitch holder. *76(86,96) sts*
Working in the round, K 12 rounds.
Change to 3.25mm (US 4) double-pointed needles and K 4 rounds.
Cast off loosely.

CHART

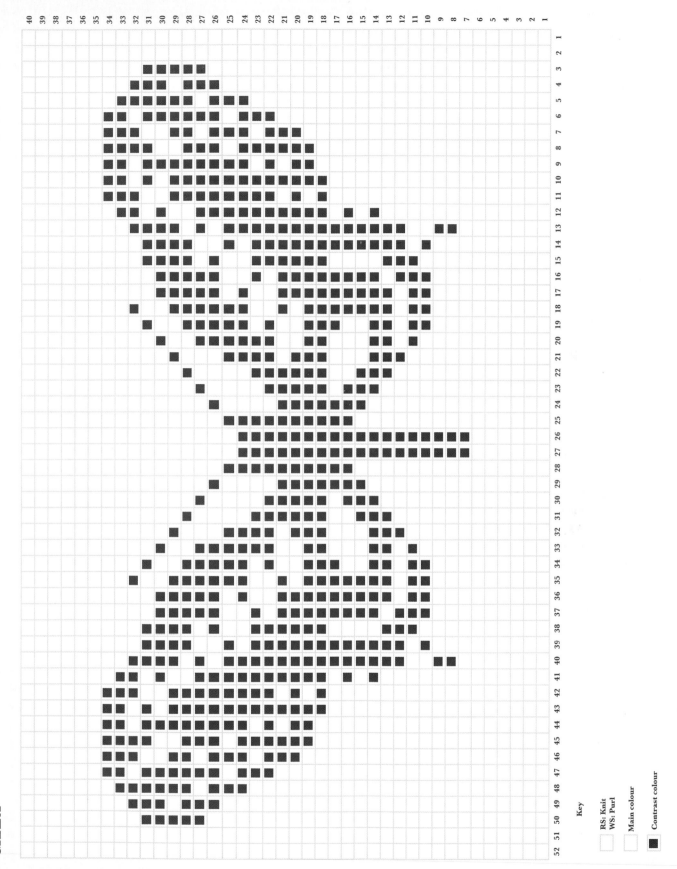

Key

RS: Knit
WS: Purl
☐ Main colour
■ Contrast colour

Cross-over Cardigan

LEFT FRONT
With 3mm (US 2/3) needles and CC1, cast on
63(67,71) sts.
K 2 rows.
Change to 3.25mm (US 3) needles and MC.
Beg with a K row, work 3 rows in st st.
Row 6 P4, cast off 4 sts, P to end.
Row 7 K to last 4 sts, cast on 4 sts, K4.
Work 3 rows in st st.
Beg working the left front chart for the flower pattern and,
at the same time, dec on the front edge on RS rows:
Row 11 Work pattern to last 4 sts, K2tog, K2.
62(66,70) sts
Row 12 P.
Rep last 2 rows until 44(45,46) sts remain, ending on a
WS row.

Shape armhole
Next row (RS) Cast off 4(5,5) sts, pattern to last 4 sts,
K2tog, K2. *39(39,40) sts*
Place a stitch marker/coloured yarn at the beg of last row,
for setting in the sleeve.
Keeping the armhole edge straight, cont to dec on the
front edge on each RS row until 20 sts remain.
Work 5(9,13) rows straight.

Shape shoulder
Next row (RS) Cast off 10 sts, K to end.
Next row P.
Cast off rem 10 sts.

RIGHT FRONT

Work as for left front, reversing shaping and following the right front chart, substituting K2tog with skpo.

BACK

With 3mm (US 2/3) needles and CC1, cast on 75(79,83) sts.
K 2 rows.
Change to 3.25mm (US 3) needles and MC.
Beg with a K row, work in st st until back measures the same as front up to the armhole shaping.

Shape armholes

Cast off 4(5,5) sts at beg of next 2 rows. *67(69,73) sts*
Work 28(32,36) rows straight.
Work the 20 rows of the back chart for the flower pattern.

Shape shoulders

Cast off 10 sts at beg of next 4 rows.
Slip remaining 27(29,33) sts onto a stitch holder.

Place a stitch marker 26(28,30)cm/10¼(11,11¾)in down from shoulder shaping, this denotes armholes

SLEEVES

With 3mm (US 2/3) needles and CC1, cast on 38(42,42) sts.
K 2 rows.
Change to 3.25mm (US 3) needles and MC.
Beg with a K row, work 8 rows in st st.
Next row (inc row) K2, M1, K to last 2 sts, M1, K2.
Work 3 rows in st st.
Rep last 4 rows until there are 64(70,74) sts.
Cont straight until sleeve measures 24(29,38)cm/9½(11½,15)in.
Place a stitch marker or coloured yarn each side of sleeve, then work another 2cm/¾in.
Cast off.

BANDS

With RS facing, 3mm (US 2/3) needles and CC1, pick up and K98(108,118) sts from right front edge, K27(29,33) sts from the back stitch holder, then pick up and K98(108,118) sts from left front edge. *223(245,269) sts*
K 1 row.
Cast off.

BUTTONHOLE FLOWER PETALS (make 5)

With 3.25mm (US 3) needles and CC1, cast on 7 sts.
K 1 row.
Row 2 PFB, P5, PFB. *9 sts*
Row 3 K1, KFB, [K2, KFB] twice, K1. *12 sts*
Beg with a P row, work 5 rows in st st.
Row 9 K1, skpo, K6, K2tog, K1. *10 sts*
Row 10 P.
Row 11 K1, skpo, K4, K2tog, K1. *8 sts*
Row 12 P.
Row 13 K1, skpo, K2, K2tog, K1. *6 sts*
Row 14 P.
Row 15 K1, skpo, K2tog, K1. *4 sts*
Row 16 P2tog twice.
Row 17 K2tog and fasten off.

COVERED BUTTON

With 3mm (US 2/3) needles and CC2, cast on 5 sts.
Work 8 rows in st st.

Cover the button (see page 120) and sew into place.

TO MAKE UP

Block and press work.

Using mattress st, join shoulder seams.

Sew the sleeves into the armholes, matching the stitch markers/yarn to the sides of the body.

Sew the side and the sleeve seams.

Sew one button to the inside of the right front to correspond with the buttonhole.

Sew the 5 flower petals around the right front buttonhole, and sew the covered button onto the left front to correspond.

Using CC2, sew 3 French knots (see page 122) in the centre of each flower.

LEFT FRONT

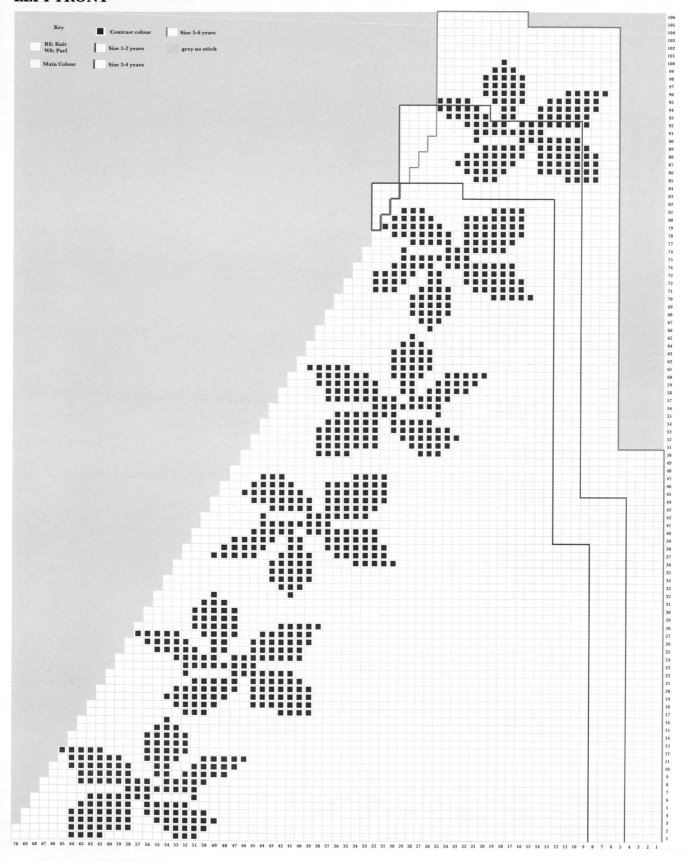

RIGHT FRONT

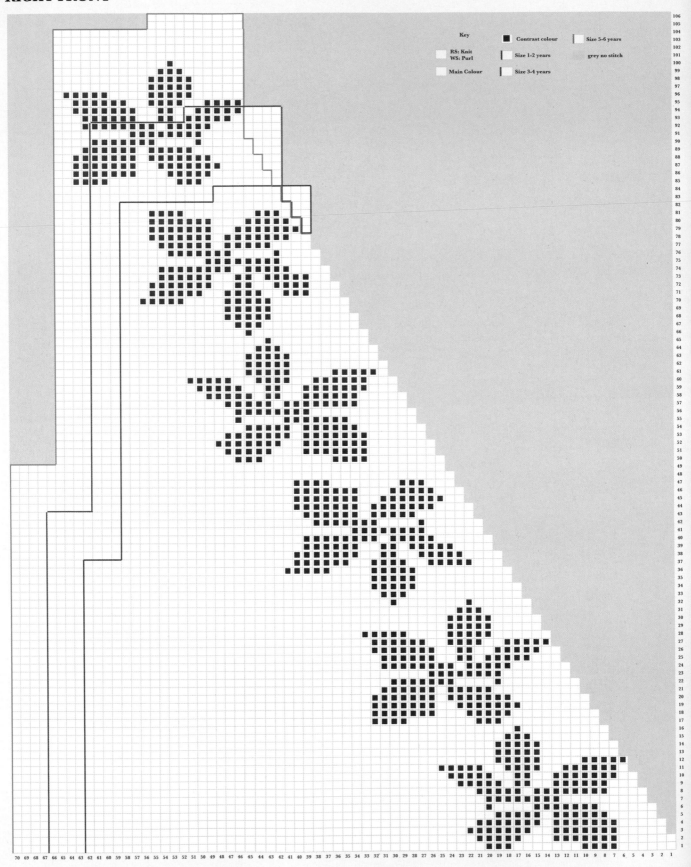

BACK

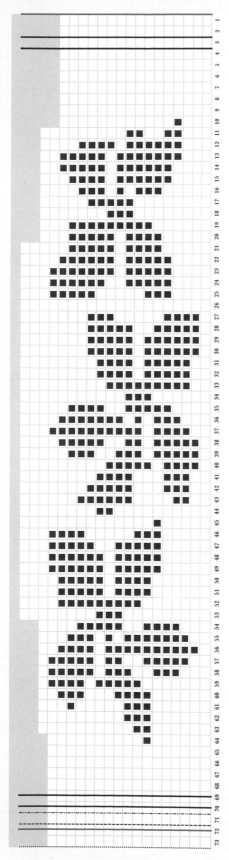

Cross-over Cardigan

Garter Stitch Version

You will need

SIZE
1–2(3–4,5–6) years

Actual chest circumference: 60(63,66)cm
/23½(24¾,26)in

YARN
Rooster *Baby Rooster*
4(5,6) x 50g/1¾oz balls in main colour
(Vintage Rose)

NEEDLES
Pair each of 3mm (US 2/3) and 3.25mm
(US 3) knitting needles

Removable stitch markers

EXTRAS
Buttons: 1 x 15mm/½in plain button
Bias binding: 150cm/59in

TENSION
25 sts and 44 rows to 10cm/4in square
over garter st using 3.25mm (US 3) needles

NOTE
Pattern is worked in garter st throughout

LEFT FRONT
With 3mm (US 2/3) needles, cast on 63(67,71) sts.
K 2 rows.
Change to 3.25 (US 3) needles and K 3 rows.
Row 6 (buttonhole) K4, cast off 4 sts, K to end.
Row 7 K to last 4 sts, cast on 4 sts, K4.
K 3 rows.
Row 11 (RS) K to last 4 sts, K2tog, K2. *62(66,70) sts*
Row 12 K.
Rep last 2 rows until work measures
13(14,15)cm/5(5¼,5½)in, ending on a WS row.

Shape armholes
Next row Cast off 4(5,5) sts, K to last 4 sts, K2tog, K2.
Keeping the armhole edge straight, cont to dec on the
front edge until 20 sts remain.
Work straight until armhole measures
13(13.5,14)cm/5(5¼,5½)in, ending on a WS row.

Shape shoulder
Next row (RS) Cast off 10 sts, K to end.
Next row P.
Cast off rem 10 sts

RIGHT FRONT

With 3mm (US 2/3) needles, cast on 63(67,71) sts.
K 2 rows.
Change to 3.25 needles and K 8 rows.
Work as for left front from Row 11, reversing shaping and substituting K2tog with skpo.

BACK

With 3mm (US 2/3) needles, cast on 75(79,83) sts.
K 2 rows.
Change to 3.25 (US 3) needles and work straight in garter st until back measures same as front up to the armhole shaping.

Shape armholes

Cast off 4(5,5) sts at beg of next 2 rows. *67(69,73) sts*
Work straight until armholes measure the same as the front armholes.

Shape shoulders

Cast off 10 sts at beg of next 4 rows.
Cast off rem 27(29,33) sts.

SLEEVES

With 3mm (US 2/3), cast on 38(42,42) sts.
K 2 rows.
Change to 3.25 (US 3) needles and K 8 rows.
Next row (inc row) K2, M1, K to last 2 sts, M1, K2. *40(44,44) sts*
K 4 rows.
Rep last 5 rows until there are 64(70,74) sts.
Cont straight in garter st until sleeve measures 27(28.5,33)cm/10¾(11¼,13)in.
Place a stitch marker or coloured yarn each side of sleeve, then work another 2cm/¾in.
Cast off.

TO MAKE UP

Block and press work.
Using mattress st, join shoulder seams.
Sew the sleeves into the armholes matching the stitch markers/yarn to the sides of the body.
Sew the right side seam and both the sleeve seams.

FOR THE FABRIC TIE

Using a piece of bias binding (see page 121) approx. 30cm/11¾in long, fold the first 3cm/1¼in of the binding lengthways with the RSs of the fabric together, pin, then sew approx. 1cm/½in from the raw edge, trim the seam.
Turn the tie the right way out and press.
Sew one side of the bias binding to the right-hand side of the cardigan, beg at the tie end of the binding and the lower right front edge of garment.
Turn the bias binding to the inside of the cardigan and slip st into place.
With approx. 30cm/11¾in of bias, sew another tie as before.
Sew the second tie into the left-hand side seam to correspond with the first tie, then join the left side seam.
Sew a button on the inside of the right front to correspond with the buttonhole.

Headband

You will need

SIZE
One size

YARN
Rooster *Baby Rooster*
1 x 50g/1¾oz ball in main colour *(Vintage Rose)* and small amounts in 2 contrast colours *(Parma Violet & Cupcake)*

NEEDLES
Pair each of 3mm (US ½) and 3.25mm (US 3) knitting needles

EXTRAS
Buttons: 1 x 18mm/¾in button

TENSION
25 sts and 34 rows to 10cm/4in square over st st using 3.25mm (US 3) needles

ABBREVIATIONS
PFB – P into the front and back of the st
KFB – K into the front and back of the st

HEADBAND
With 3.25mm (US 3) needles and MC, cast on 135 sts.
K 2 rows.
Beg with a K row, work 9 rows in st st.
K 2 rows.
Cast off.

FLOWER PETALS (make 5)
With 3.25mm (US 3) needles and CC1, cast on 7 sts.
K 1 row.
Row 2 PFB, P5, PFB. *9 sts*
Row 3 K1, KFB, [K2, KFB] twice, K1. *12 sts*
Beg with a P row, work 5 rows in st st.
Row 9 K1, skpo, K6, K2tog, K1. *10 sts*
Row 10 P.
Row 11 K1, skpo, K4, K2tog, K1. *8 sts*
Row 12 P.
Row 13 K1, skpo, K2, K2tog, K1. *6 sts*
Row 14 P.
Row 15 K1, skpo, K2tog, K1. *4 sts*
Row 16 P2tog twice.
Row 17 K2tog and fasten off.

COVERED BUTTON FOR FLOWER CENTRE

With 3mm (US 2/3) needles and CC2, cast on 5 sts.
Work 8 rows in st st.
Cover the button (see page 120) and sew into place.

TO MAKE UP

Block and press work, overlap the two ends of the
headband, adjust to fit child and sew ends together.
Arrange the petals in a circle and sew into place on
headband overlap.
Sew covered button into centre of the flower.

Dress

FRONT
For the dress with knitted skirt
With 3.25mm (US 3) needles and CC, cast on 120(130,146) sts.
K 1 row.
Change to MC and beg with K row, work 10(12,14) rows in st st.
Next row (dec row – RS) K31(33,35), s2kpo, K62(66,70), s2kpo, K rem 31(33,35) sts. *116(126,142) sts*
Work 11(13,15) rows in st st.
Next dec row K30(32,34), s2kpo, K60(64,68), s2kpo, K rem 30(32,34) sts. *112(122,138) sts*
Work 11(13,15) rows in st st.
Next dec row K29(31,33), s2kpo, K58(62,66), s2kpo, K rem 29(31,33) sts. *108(118,134) sts*
Work 11(13,15) rows in st st.

Next dec row K28(30,32), s2kpo, K56(60,64), s2kpo, K rem 28(30,32) sts. *104(114,130) sts*
Work 11(13,15) rows in st st.
Next dec row K27(29,31), s2kpo, K54(58,62), s2kpo, K rem 27(29,31) sts. *100(110,126) sts*
Cont in this manner, but now dec every 6th row 6(6,8) more times. *76(86,94) sts*
Work straight until skirt measures 32(38,42)cm /12½(15,17¼)in or required skirt length, ending on a WS row.
Change to CC.
Cont pattern from ***.

For the dress with fabric skirt
*With 3.25mm (US 3) needles and CC, cast on 76(86,94) sts.
Cont pattern from ***.

*** Bodice
K 2 rows.
Beg with a K row, work 9 rows in st st.
Next row (WS) K.
Change to MC and work 3(5,7)cm/1¼(2,2¾)in in st st, ending on a WS row.

Shape armholes
Cast off 3 sts at beg of next 2 rows.
Cast off 2 sts at beg of next 2 rows. *66(76,84) sts*
Dec 1 st at beg of every row until 54(64,70) sts remain. **

Work straight until armhole measures 7(7.5,8)cm /2¾(3,3¾)in, ending on a WS row.

Divide for neck and shoulders
Row 1 K22(26,29), cast off 10(12,12) sts, K to end.

Right shoulder (work each shoulder separately)
Dec 1 st on every row at neck edge until 12(16,19) sts remain.
Work straight until armhole measures 13(13.5,14)cm /5(5¼,5½)in.
Cast off.

Left shoulder
With WS facing, re-join yarn to left shoulder sts as work as for right shoulder.

BACK
For the dress with knitted skirt: Work as for front to **.
For the dress with fabric skirt: Work as for front from * to **.
Work straight until armhole measures 9(9.5,10)cm /3½(3¾,4)in, ending on a WS row.
Divide for neck and shoulders
Row 1 K22(26,29), cast off 10(12,12) sts, K to end.

Left shoulder (work each shoulder separately)
Dec 1 st on every row at neck edge until 12(16,19) sts remain.
Work straight until armhole measures 15(15.5,16)cm /6(6,6¼)in, ending on a WS row.
Next row (buttonhole row – RS) K2(3,3), yf, K2tog, K4(6,9), K2tog, yf, K2(3,3).
Work 2 rows.
Cast off.

Right shoulder
With WS facing, re-join yarn to right shoulder sts as work as for left shoulder.

BOW
For the dress with knitted skirt
With 3.25 (US 3) needles and CC, cast on 12 sts.
Work 15cm/6in in garter st.
Cast off.
For the dress with fabric skirt
With 3.25 (US 3) needles and CC, cast on 8 sts.
Work 10cm/4in in garter st.
Cast off.

TO MAKE UP
Block and press work.
Sew side seams together.

Bands for dress with knitted skirt
For all the bands, use 3mm (US 2/3) needles and CC, and beg with RS facing.
Left armhole
Beg at the neck edge of the buttonhole band and ending at the neck edge of the button band, pick up and K into every st.
Cast off.

Right armhole
Beg at the neck edge of the button band and ending at the neck edge of the buttonhole band, pick up and K into every st.
Cast off.

Front neck
Pick up and K into every st.
Cast off.

Back neck
Pick up and K into every st.
Cast off.

Bands for dress with fabric skirt
For all the bands, use 3mm (US 2/3) needles and MC, and beg with RS facing.
Left armhole
Beg at the shoulder edge of the buttonhole band and ending at the shoulder edge of the button band, pick up and K into every st.
Cast off.
Right armhole
Beg at the shoulder edge of the button band and ending at the shoulder edge of the buttonhole band, pick up and K into every st.
Cast off.
Front neck
Beg at the neck edge and ending at the neck edge, pick up and K into every st.
Cast off.
Back neck
Beg at the neck edge and ending at the neck edge, pick up and K into every st.
Cast off.

TO MAKE THE COVERED BUTTONS
For the dress with knitted dress
With 2.25mm (US 1) needles and CC, cast on 5 sts.
Work 5 rows in st st.
Cast off.
Cover the button (see page 120) and sew into place.

For the dress with fabric skirt
Cut 3, 15mm/½in circles from the fabric.
Cover the button and sew into place.

Fabric skirt
To make the fabric skirt follow the instructions for the Long-Sleeved Dress skirt (see pages 29–31).

Holyrood

Holyrood Palace was the principle residence of the Kings and Queens of Scotland, and famously was once the home of Mary Queen of Scots. It is now the official residence of the British monarch in Scotland, and the Queen spends one week at Holyrood at the beginning of every summer to carry out a range of official duties and ceremonies.

The Holyrood Collection has a range of tough, warm garments that are thick enough to combat the roughest of weathers. There are lots of texture and hints of plaid to pay homage to its Scottish roots but also some clean smooth pieces too, to echo the smooth Holyrood stone.

Cabled Sweater

You will need

SIZE
1–2(2–3,3–4) years

Actual chest circumference 59(62,66)cm
/23¼(24½,26)in

YARN
Millamia *Naturally Soft Merino*
5(6,7) x 50g/1¾oz balls in main colour
(Forget Me Not)
1 x 50g/1¾oz ball in contrast colour
(Midnight) for the knitted shoulder pads

NEEDLES
Pair each of 3mm (US2/3) and 3.25mm
(US 3) knitting needles
Stitch holders

TENSION
25 sts and 34 rows to 10cm/4in square
over st st using 3.25mm (US 3) needles

EXTRAS
For the knitted shoulder pads: 4(4,4) buttons
For the fabric shoulder pads: piece of
fabric 45 x 18cm/18 x 7in and 3(4,4)
buttons

ABBREVIATIONS
C2F – cable 2 front – slip next 2 sts onto a cable needle
and hold at front of the work, K2, K2 from cable needle
C2B – cable 2 back – slip next 2 sts onto a cable needle
and hold at back of the work, K2, K2 from cable needle.

CABLE PANEL (34 sts)
Row 1 P2, K4, P2, K1, P1, K1, P2, K8, P2, K1, P1,
K1, P2, K4, P2.
Row 2 K2, P4, K2, P1, K1, P1, K2, P8, K2, P1, K1, P1,
K2, P4, K2.
Row 3 P2, C2F, P3, K1, P3, C2F, C2B, P3, K1, P3,
C2F, P2.
Row 4 K2, P4, K3, P1, K3, P8, K3, P1, K3, P4, K2.
Row 5 As Row 1.
Row 6 As Row 2.
Row 7 P2, K4, P3, K1, P3, C2B, C2F, P3, K1, P3,
K4, P2.
Row 8 As Row 4.
Row 9 P2, C2F, P2, K1, P1, K1, P2, K8, P2, K1, P1, K1,
P2, C2F, P2.
Row 10 As Row 2.
Row 11 P2, K4, P3, K1, P3, C2F, C2B, P3, K1, P3,
K4, P2.
Row 12 As Row 4.
Row 13 As Row 1.
Row 14 As Row 2.

Row 15 P2, C2F, P3, K1, P3, C2B, C2F, P3, K1, P3, C2F, P2.
Row 16 As Row 4.
Row 17 As Row 1.
Row 18 As Row 2.
Row 19 P2, K4, P3, K1, P3, C2F, C2B, P3, K1, P3, K4, P2.
Row 20 As Row 4.
Row 21 P2, C2F, P2, K1, P1, K1, P2, K8, P2, K1, P1, K1, P2, C2F, P2.
Row 22 As Row 2.
Row 23 P2, K4, P3, K1, P3, C2B, C2F, P3, K1, P3, K4, P2.
Row 24 As Row 4.
These 24 rows set the cable pattern.

BACK
With 3mm (US 2/3) needles and CC, cast on 82(86,94) sts.
K 2 rows.
Change to MC and work in K1, P1 rib for 2cm/¾in, ending on a WS row
Change to 3.25mm (US 3) needles.
Next row Moss st 24(26,30), work Row 1 of the cable pattern, moss st to end.
Cont to work the cable panel with 24(26,30) sts of moss st either side until back measures 18.5(20.5,24)cm /7¼(8,9½)in or required length, ending on a WS row.

Shape armholes
Cast off 5 sts at beg of next 2 rows. *72(76,84) sts*
Cont to keep pattern correct, dec 1 st at each end of next and every foll alt row until 60(64,72) sts remain. **
Work straight until back measures 33(36,40)cm /13(14¼,15¾)in from cast-on edge, ending on a WS row.

Divide for neck and shoulders
Next row (RS) Work 13(14,17) sts, turn and work on these sts only (leaving rem sts on a stitch holder).

Right shoulder
Work 1 row in moss st.
Cast off 7 sts at beg of next row (armhole edge).
Work 1 row in moss st.
Cast off remaining 6(7,10) sts.

Left shoulder
Slip the centre 34(36,38) sts (neck sts) onto a stitch holder.
With RS facing, re-join yarn at neck edge and work to end.
Cast off 7 sts at beg of next row (armhole edge).
Work 1 row in moss st.
Cast off rem 6(7,10) sts.

FRONT
Work as for back to **.
Cont in pattern until front measures 28(31,34)cm /11(12¼,13½)in, ending on a WS row.

Divide for neck and shoulders
Next row (RS) Work 26(28,32) sts, turn and work on these sts only (leaving rem sts on a stitch holder).

Left shoulder
Next row K2tog (neck edge), work to end. *25(27,31) sts*
Next row Work to last 2 sts, K2tog. *24(26,30) sts*
Rep last 2 rows until 13(14,17) sts remain.
Work straight until front measures the same as back to shoulder shaping, ending at the armhole edge.
Cast off 7 sts at beg of next row.
Work 1 row in pattern.
Cast off rem 6(7,10) sts.

Right shoulder
Slip centre 8 sts (neck sts) onto a stitch holder.
With RS facing, re-join yarn at neck edge and work the right neck and shoulder as the left, reversing shaping.

SLEEVES (make 2)
With 3mm (US 2/3) needles and CC, cast on 48(50,52) sts.
K 2 rows.
Change to MC and work in K1, P1 rib for 3cm/1¼in, ending on a WS row.
Change to 3.25mm (US 3) needles.
Next row Moss st 7(8,9), work Row 1 of the cable pattern, moss st to end.
Work 1 row in pattern.
Keeping the pattern of the central cable panel with moss st borders correct, inc 1 st at each end of next and every foll 6th row until there are 68(70,72) sts.

Work straight until the sleeve measures 17(20,24)cm/6¾(8,9½)in or required length, ending on a WS row.

Cast off 5 sts at beg of next 2 rows. *58(60,62) sts*
Dec 1 st at each end of every RS row until 50 sts remain.
Cast off 4 sts at beg of next 4 rows. *34 sts*
Cast off 4 sts at beg of next 6 rows.
Cast off rem 10 sts. ***

NECK BAND

Join right shoulder seam.

With 3mm (US 2/3) needles and MC and beg at the left shoulder, cast on 6 sts, pick up and K into every st from left front neck, K8 sts from front stitch holder, pick up and K into every st from right front neck, pick and K into every st from right back neck, K34(36,38) sts from back stitch holder, and finally pick up and K into every st from back left neck. Ensure you have an even number of sts.

Work 3 rows in K1, P1 rib.

Next row (buttonhole row – RS) Rib 3, yf, K2tog, rib to end.

Rib 3 rows.

Change to CC and K 1 row.

Cast off in CC.

SHOULDER PADS

Right shoulder pad

With 3mm (US 2/3) needles and CC, cast on 41(43,45) sts.

K 2 rows.

Next row K18(19,20), P2, K1, P2, K18(19,20).

Next row K2tog, P16(17,18), K2, P1, K2, P16(17,18), K2tog. *39(41,43) sts*

Rep last 2 rows until 21 sts remain.

Cast off.

Left shoulder pad – front

With 3mm (US 2/3) needles and CC, cast on 23(24,25) sts.

K 2 rows.

Row 3 K to last 5 sts, P2, K1, P2.

Row 4 (buttonhole row) K2, yf, K2tog, K1, P to last 2 sts, K2tog. *22(23,24) sts*

Row 5 As Row 3.

Row 6 K2, P1, K2, P to last 2 sts, K2tog. *21(22,23) sts*

Rows 7–10 Rep Rows 5 & 6 twice more. *19(20,21) sts*

Rep Rows 3 to 10 once more. *15(16,17) sts*

Rep Rows 3 & 4 once. *13(14,15) sts*

2nd and 3rd size only Rep Rows 5 & 6 until 13 sts remain.

All sizes Rep Row 5 once.

Cast off rem 13 sts.

Left shoulder pad - back

With 3mm (US 2/3) needles and CC, cast on 21(22,23) sts.

K 2 rows.

Row 1 K.

Row 2 K2tog, P to last 3 sts K3. *20(21,22) sts*

Rep last 2 rows until 11 sts remain.

Cast off.

TO MAKE UP

Block and press work.

Join the very end of the left shoulder seam for approx. 1cm/½in from the arm edge.

Fold sleeves in half, marry the fold with the shoulder seam and sew the sleeves into place.

Join the sleeve and side seams.

Sew the right shoulder pad into place, placing the middle rib to the shoulder seam (the pads should have reverse stocking stitch to the RS).

Tack the left back and front shoulder pads together, overlapping the rib with the garter st button band, then pin the pad into place so that it spans the shoulder. Sew into place and remove the tacking stitches.

Sew buttons into place to correspond with the buttonholes.

FOR THE SWEATER WITH FABRIC SHOULDER PADS

Work as for main pattern until *** is reached, working all rows in MC only.

Left front shoulder edge

With 3mm (US 2/3) needles and RS facing, pick up and K into every stitch on the left front shoulder.

K 1 row.

Cast off.

Neck band

Join right shoulder seam.

With 3mm (US 2/3) needles and beg at the left shoulder, pick up and K 2 sts from the end of the shoulder edge, pick up and K into every st from left front neck, K8 sts from front stitch holder, pick up and K into every st from right front neck, pick and K into every st from right back neck, K34(36,38) sts from back stitch holder, and finally pick up and K into every st from back left neck. Ensure you have an even number of sts.

Work 7 rows in K1, P1 rib.

Cast off in rib.

TO MAKE UP

Block and press work.

Join the very end of the left shoulder seam for approx. 0.5cm/¼in from the arm edge.

Fold sleeves in half, marry the fold with the shoulder seam and sew the sleeves into place.

Join the sleeve and side seams.

Fabric shoulder pads

Place the fabric onto a flat surface and then place another piece of fabric for the lining on top of the main fabric, pin the shoulder pad guide onto the fabric and cut out making sure that the straight grain line is on the straight grain of the fabric so that the shoulder pads are cut on the cross grain.

Place and refer to pattern pieces (see pages 86–87). With right sides of the fabric and lining facing sew a small seam around the edge, leaving the neck edge open.

Turn to the right side and press, sew the shoulder pads into place folding the neck to the inside to neaten off.

Make 3(4,4) loops (see page 123) on the front left shoulder edge.

Sew buttons to correspond with the button loops.

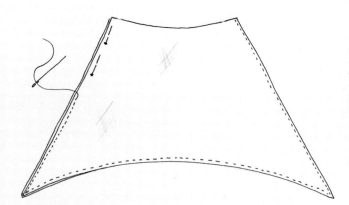

**SHOULDER PAD GUIDE
(RIGHT SHOULDER)**

Note: These guides are to scale
and can be copied at 100%

SIZE 2–3

SIZE 3–4

SIZE 1–2

SIZE 2–3

SIZE 3–4

SHOULDER PAD GUIDE
(LEFT SHOULDER) MAKE 2

Note: These guides are to scale and can be copied at 100%

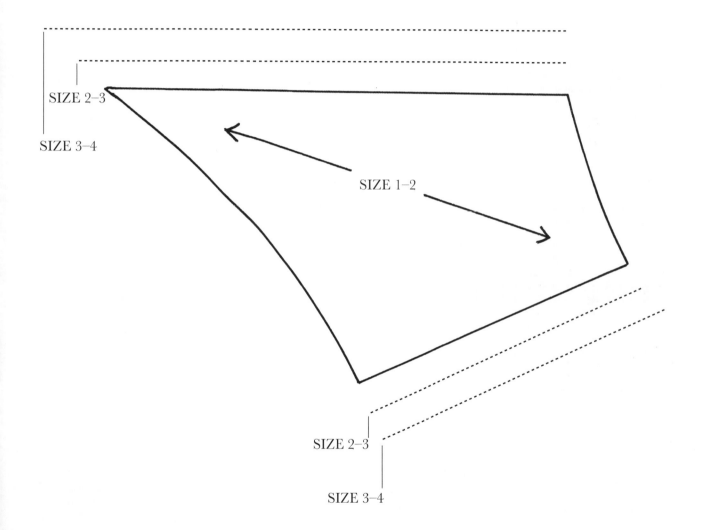

SIZE 2–3

SIZE 3–4

SIZE 1–2

SIZE 2–3

SIZE 3–4

Gilet

Garter Stitch & Patterned Versions

You will need

SIZE
1–2(2–3,3–4) years

Actual chest circumference 59(62,66)cm
/23¼(24½,26)in

YARN
Millamia *Naturally Soft Merino*
For the patterned version:
6(6,7) x 50g/1¾oz balls in main colour
(Forget Me Not)
1 x 50g/1¾oz ball each of 2 contrasting
colours for main garment *(Midnight
& Snow)*
6(6,7,7) x 50g/1¾oz balls for the lining.
For the garter st version:
6(6,7) x 50g/1¾oz balls in main colour
(Forget Me Not)
1 x 50g/1¾oz ball of contrast colour
(Midnight).

NEEDLES
Pair each of 2.75mm (US 2) and 3.25mm
(US 3) knitting needles.

TENSION
25 sts and 34 rows to 10cm/4in square
over st st using 3.25mm (US 3) needles

EXTRAS
Buttons: For the patterned version: 5(6,6) buttons
For the garter st version: 5(5,6) buttons
For the garter st version: 0.5m/½yd of fabric, and
matching thread.

ABBREVIATIONS
C2F – cable 2 front – slip next 2 sts onto a cable needle
and hold at front of the work, K2, K2 from cable needle
C2B – cable 2 back – slip next 2 sts onto a cable needle
and hold at back of the work, K2, K2 from cable needle.

NOTE
For the garter st version, work as for the patterned
version, but using garter st and main colour yarn
throughout.

HOOD (make 2)
With 3.25mm (US 3) needles and MC, cast on 3 sts.
Working in st st, follow the pattern chart (see page 94),
introducing the CC1 and CC2 and increasing 1 st at each
end of every RS row until the sides of the hood measure
25(27,28)cm/9¾(10½,11)in, ending on a WS row.
Working in MC only, dec 1 st at each end of every RS
row until 3 sts remain.
Cast off.

BACK

With 3.25mm (US 3) needles and MC, cast on
74(80,86) sts.

Beg with a K row, work 11 rows in st st.

Next row K. (This forms the turn of the hem.)
Work 4 rows in st st.

Following the chart (see page 93), work the border
pattern then cont in st st with MC only until the back
measures 18(21,24)cm/7(8¼,9½)in, ending on a
WS row.

Shape armholes

Cast off 3(3,4) sts at beg of next 2 rows. *68(74,78) sts*

Next row K2, K2tog tbl, K to last 4 sts, K2tog, K2.
66(72,76) sts

Next row P.

Rep last 2 rows until 56(60,64) sts remain.

Work straight until back measures 30(34,38)cm
/11¾(13½,15)in, ending on a WS row.

Shape shoulders

Cast off 6(7,7) sts at beg of next 2 rows. *44(46,50) sts*

Cast off 7(7,8) sts at beg of foll 2 rows.

Cast off rem 30(32,34) sts off loosely.

LEFT FRONT

With 3.25 needles (US 3) and MC, cast on
33(36,39) sts.

Beg with a K row, work 11 rows in st st.

Next row K. (This forms the turn of the hem.)
Work 4 rows in st st.

Following the chart, work the border pattern then
cont in st st with MC only until the front measures
18(21,24)cm/7(8¼,9½)in, ending at armhole edge.

Shape armholes

Cast off 3(3,4) sts at beg of next row. *30(33,35) sts*

Next row P.

Next row K2, K2tog tbl, K to end. *29(32,34) sts*

Next row P.

Rep last 2 rows until 24(26,28) sts remain.

Work straight until front measures 28(31,35)cm
/11(12½,13¾)in, ending at neck edge.

Shape neck

Cast off 8(8,9) sts at beg of next row. *16(18,19) sts*

Next row K to last 4 sts, K2tog, K2. *15(17,18) sts*

Next row P.

Rep last 2 rows until 13(14,15) sts remain.

Work straight until front measures the same as back
to the shoulder shaping, ending at armhole edge.

Shape shoulder

Cast off 6(7,7) sts at beg of next row.

Work 1 row.

Cast off remaining 7(7,8) sts.

RIGHT FRONT

Work as for the left front, reversing shaping and
substituting K2tog for K2tog tbl on armhole and
neck shaping.

KNITTED LINING

HOOD (make 2)

With 3.25mm (US 3) needles and MC, cast on 3 sts.

Working in st st, inc 1 st at each end of every RS row
until the sides of the hood measure 25(27,28)cm
/9¾(10½,11)in, ending on a WS row.

Dec 1 st each end of every RS row until 3 sts remain.
Cast off.

BACK

With 3.25 (US 3) needles and MC, cast on
74(80,86) sts.

Work straight in st st until the back measures
17(20,23)cm/6¾(7¾,9)in, ending on a WS row.

Shape armholes

Cast off 3(3,4) sts at beg of next 2 rows. *68(74,78) sts*

Next row K2, K2tog tbl, K to last 4 sts, K2tog, K2.
66(72,76) sts

Next row P.

Rep last 2 rows until 56(60,64) sts remain.

Work straight until back measures 29(33,37)cm
/11½(13,14½)in, ending on a WS row.

Shape shoulders

Cast off 6(7,7) sts at beg of next 2 rows. *44(46,50) sts*

Cast off 7(7,8) sts at beg of foll 2 rows.

Cast remaining 30(32,34) sts off loosely.

RIGHT FRONT

With 3.25 (US 3) needles and MC, cast on
33(36,39) sts.

Work in st st until the front measures 17(20,23)cm
/6¾(7¾,9)in, ending at armhole edge.

Shape armholes

Cast off 3(3,4) sts at beg of next row. *30(33,35) sts*

Next row P.

Next row K2, K2tog tbl, K to end. *29(32,34) sts*
Next row P.
Rep last 2 rows until 24(26,28) sts remain.
Work straight until front measures 27(30,34)cm /10¾(11¾,13½)in, ending at neck edge.

Shape neck

Cast off 8(8,9) sts at beg of next row. *16(18,19) sts*
Next row K to last 4 sts, K2tog, K2. *15(17,18) sts*
Next row P.
Rep last 2 rows until 13(14,15) sts remain.
Cont straight until front measures the same as back from armhole to shoulder shaping, ending at the armhole edge.

Shape shoulder

Cast off 6(7,7) sts at beg of next row.
Work 1 row.
Cast off remaining 7(7,8) sts.

LEFT FRONT

Work as for the right front, reversing shaping and substituting K2tog for K2tog tbl on armhole and neck shaping.

BANDS FOR GARTER ST VERSION
ARMHOLE BANDS

Join the shoulder seams.
With 2.75mm (US 2) needles, CC and RS facing, beg at the underarm, pick up and K 64(70,76) sts from all around the armhole.
Next row K.
Work 3 more rows in reverse st st.
Cast off.

Right band – button band

With 3.25mm (US 3) needles, MC and RS facing, beg 3.5cm/1½in above the right bottom edge, pick up and K 64(70,76) sts up to the neck edge.
K 11 rows.
Cast off loosely.
With stitch markers or coloured yarn, evenly mark 5(5,6) positions for the buttons.

Left band – buttonhole band

Work as for the button band, beg at the left neck edge and finishing 3.5cm/1½in above the bottom edge.
K 5 rows in.

Next row Make a button hole at each of the button markers (yf, K2tog).
K 5 rows.
Cast off loosely.

HOOD EDGING FOR GARTER ST VERSION

With 2.75mm (US 2) needles, CC and RS facing, beg at right neck edge, pick up and K 130(140,150) sts from all around the hood.
Next row K.
Work 3 more rows in reverse stocking st.
Cast off.

FABRIC LINING

Block and press work
Lay each of the knitted pieces onto the fabric (RSs together) and, leaving 3cm/1¼in ease/seam allowance around each edge, cut out the lining.

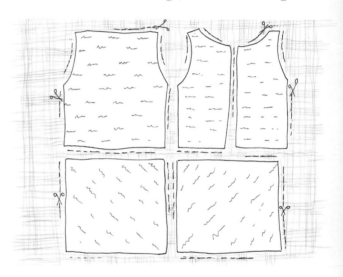

With RSs together, sew the fabric hood on two edges (A) and sew the side and shoulder seams on the main body (B). Press the seams open.

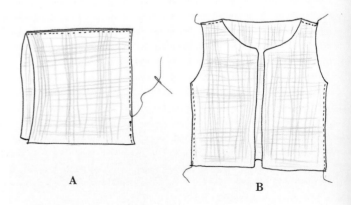

A   B

Run a row of gathering stitches along the neck edge of the hood (C).

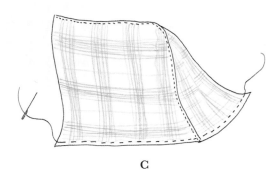

C

Ease the hood onto the body lining and snip along the neck seam.

Place the lining inside the gilet with WSs together.

Using little running sts, sew the lining into place at the edge of the MC.

Turn the contrast edging to the inside and slip st into place. Sew the armhole bands into place in the same manner.

Fold the front edge of the lining inside and slip st into place down each side.

Turn the bottom 3.5cm/1½in over the lining to form a hem and slip st into place (D).

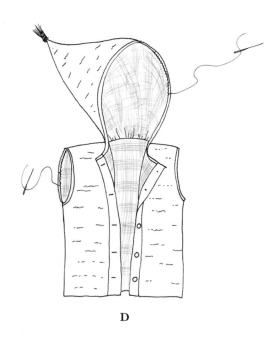

D

FRONT BANDS FOR PATTERNED VERSION
Right band – button band

With 2.75mm (US 2) needles, MC and RS facing, beg at the knit row at lower right edge (leaving the hem free), cast on 4 sts, pick up and K86(98,110) sts, cast on 4 sts. *94(106,118) sts*

When working the different colours, always keeping the spare yarns to the WS of the work

Next row K4 (MC), *K2 (MC), P2 (CC1), K2 (CC2), P2 (MC), K2 (CC1), P2 (CC2),* rep from * to * to last 6 sts, K6 (MC).

Next row K4 (MC), *P2 (MC), K2 (CC2), P2 (CC1), K2 (MC), P2 (CC2), K2 (CC1),* rep from * to * to last 6 sts, P2 (MC), K4 (MC).

Rep last 2 rows 4 times more.

Cast off loosely in MC.

With stitch markers or coloured yarn, evenly mark 5(6,6) positions for the buttons.

Left band – buttonhole band

With 2.75mm (US 2) needles, MC and RS facing, beg at the upper left edge, cast on 4 sts, pick up and K86(98,110) sts, cast on 4 sts. *94(106,118) sts*

Next row K4 (MC), *K2 (MC), P2 (CC1), K2 (CC2), P2 (MC), K2 (CC1), P2 (CC2),* rep from * to * to last 6 sts, K6 (MC).

Next row K4 (MC), *P2 (MC), K2 (CC2), P2 (CC1), K2 (MC), P2 (CC2), K2 (CC1),* rep from * to * to last 6 sts, P2 (MC), K4 (MC).

Rep last 2 rows once more.

Next row (buttonhole row) Cont in rib pattern, cast off 4 sts opposite each button marker.

Next row Cont in rib pattern, cast on 4 sts over each cast-off point, keeping the colour sequence correct.

Work 4 rows in pattern.

Cast off loosely.

TO MAKE UP FOR PATTERNED VERSION BOTH FOR THE OUTSIDE AND THE LINING.

Block and press work, easing the hood pieces into squares.

Using mattress st, join the shoulder seams.

Sew the 2 squares together on two sides to form the hood, placing the patterned sides together so that the pattern comes at the point of the hood.

Ease and sew the hood onto the neck opening (there will be a slight gather along the neck edge of the hood).

Sew the side seams.

With WSs together, place the lining inside the gilet. Using mattress st, sew into place at the armholes, around the hood, and the front opening. Secure the lining at the neck seam and at the point of the hood.

Turn the hood lining to the outside so that a little border of contrast colour is formed.

Turn the bottom hems over the lining and slip st into place.

Turn the ends of the front bands to the inside and slip st into place.

Slip st around the buttonholes to keep any long yarns out of the way.

Sew buttons opposite the buttonholes.

Make a tassel and sew to the point of the hood.

TO MAKE UP FOR GARTER ST VERSION

Block and press work, easing the hood pieces into squares.

Using mattress st, join the shoulder seams.

Ease and sew the hood onto the neck opening.

Sew the two squares together on two sides to form the hood.

Sew the side seams.

Turn the ends of the front bands to the inside and slip st into place.

Sew buttons opposite the button holes.

Make a tassel and sew to the point of the hood.

TO MAKE THE TASSEL

Take a stiff piece of plastic or cardboard (a CD case is ideal).

Secure the end of the yarn with a piece of sticky tape and wind the yarn around the case, 25 to 30 times.

Thread a piece of yarn through the top edge of the wound yarn and tie a knot.

Cut through the lower end of the wound yarn.

Take another piece of yarn and wind it around the tassel to form a 'neck'.

Trim the tassel to the required length.

BODY CHART

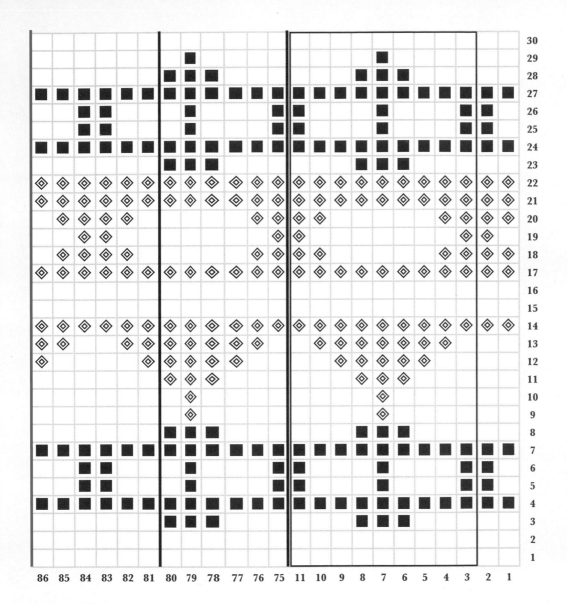

HOOD CHART

Key

RS: Knit
WS: Purl

Main colour

Contrast colour 1

Contrast colour 2

grey no stitch

Hat

You will need

SIZE
1–2(3–4,5–6) years

YARN
Millamia *Naturally Soft Merino*
2 x 50g/1¾oz balls *(Forget Me Not)*

NEEDLES
Pair each of 2.75mm (US 2) and 3.25mm
(US 3) knitting needles

TENSION
26 sts and 35 rows to 10cm/4in square
over st st using 3.25mm (US 3) needles

HAT
With 2.75mm (US 2) needles, cast on 102(110,118) sts.
Row 1 [K2, P2] to last 2 sts, K2.
Row 2 [P2, K2] to last 2 sts, P2.
Rep Rows 1 & 2 until hat measures 7(8,9)cm/2¾(3¼,3½)
in, ending on a WS row.

Change to 3.25mm (US 3) needles.
Rep Rows 1 & 2 until hat measures 18(20,22)cm
/7(7¾,8¾)in, ending on a WS row.

Next row (RS) [K2, P2tog] to last 2 sts, K2. *77(83,89) sts*
Next row [P2, K1] to last 2 sts, P2.
Next row [K2, P1] to last2 sts, K2.
Rep last 2 rows for 6(7,8)cm/2¼(2¾,3¼)in, ending on a
WS row.

Next row [K2tog, P1] to last 2 sts, K2tog. *51(55,59) sts*
Next row [P1, K1] to last st, P1
Next row [K1, P1] to last st, K1.
Rep last 2 rows for 5(6,7)cm/2(2¼,2¾)in, ending on a
WS row.

Next row K1, [K2tog] to end. *26(28,30) sts*
Next row P.
Beg with a K row, work 6 rows in st st.
Next row [K2tog] to end. *13(14,15) sts*
Next row P.
Work 13cm/5in in st st, ending with a WS row.
Next row K1(0,1), [K2tog] to end.
Next row P.
Cut yarn, thread through remaining 7(7,8) sts and
fasten off.

TO MAKE UP
Join the back seam, inverting the brim seam.
Tie a knot in the pointed end.
Fold brim back once or twice as required.

Scarf

You will need

SIZE
One size

YARN
Millamia *Naturally Soft Merino*
2 x 50g/1³⁄₄oz balls *(Forget Me Not)*

NEEDLES
Pair of 4.5mm (US 7) knitting needles

TENSION
20 sts and 33 rows to 10cm/4in square
over garter st using 4.5mm (US 7) needles
and yarn double

NOTE
Pattern is worked with 2 strands of yarn in garter
st throughout.

SCARF
With 4.5mm (US 7) needles and 2 strands of yarn,
cast on 10 sts.
K 2 rows.
Next row M1 into first st, K to end. *11 sts*
Rep last row until there are 16(20,24) sts.
Slipping first of every row, work straight until scarf
measures 8cm/3¹⁄₄in, ending on a WS row.
Next row (RS) K8(10,12), turn and work on these
sts only.
K 9(10,11) rows.
Cut yarn and leave sts on stitch holder.
With RS facing, re-join yarn to rem 8(10,12) sts.
K 10(11,12) rows, then work across the st from the
first side. *16(20,24) sts*
Work straight until scarf measures 60(65,70)cm
/23¹⁄₂(25¹⁄₂,27¹⁄₂)in or required length, ending on a
WS row.
Next row K2tog, K to end.
Rep last row until 10 sts remain.
K 2 rows.
Cast off.

Toy Mice

*These knitted mice make chic and cuddly toys, and
you can even make them a stylish wardrobe.*

Toy Mice

You will need

YARN

Rowan *Baby Merino Silk DK*

2 x 50g/1¾oz balls in main colour *(Straw)*

Small amount (approx. 20g) in pink for nose, inner ears and foot pads

NEEDLES

Pair each of 3.5mm (US 4) and 4mm (US 6) knitting needles

Stitch holders

EXTRAS

Removable stitch markers

For fabric embellished version: approx. 20cm of fabric for inner ears and foot pads, embroidery stabiliser, matching sewing thread

2 x beads or buttons for eyes or, if the mouse is for very young children, scraps of black yarn

Washable toy stuffing

TENSION

22 sts and 30 rows to 10cm/4in square over st st using 4mm (US 6) needles

---

NOTE

M1 – make/increase 1 st by knitting into both front and back of st.

M2 – make/increase 2 sts by knitting into front, back and front again of st.

HEAD

Using 4mm (US 6) needles and pink yarn, cast on 7 sts.

Row 1 (RS) M1 into every st. *14 sts*

P 1 row.

Change to MC and beg with a K row, work in st st throughout.

Work 2 rows.

Row 5 M2 into first st, K4, M2 into next st, K2, M2 into next st, K4, M2 into next st. *22 sts*

Work 3 rows.

Row 9 M2 into first st, K6, M2 into next st, K6, M2 into next st, K6, M2 into next st. *30 sts*

Work 3 rows.

Row 13 M2 into first st, K8, M2 into next st, K10, M2 into next st, K8, M2 into next st. *38 sts*
Work 3 rows.
Row 17 M2 into first st, K10, M2 into next st, K14, M2 into next st, K10, M2 into next st. *46 sts*
Work 3 rows.
Row 21 M2 into first st, K12, M2 into next st, K18, M2 into next st, K12, M2 into next st. *54 sts*
Work 3 rows
Row 25 M2 into first st, K14, M2 into next st, K22, M2 into next st, K14, M2 into next st. *62 sts*
Work 3 rows.
Row 29 M2 into first st, K16, M2 into next st, K26, M2 into next st, K16, M2 into next st. *70 sts*
Work 3 rows.
Row 33 K20, K2tog, K26, K2tog tbl, K to end. *68 sts*
Row 34 P.
Row 35 K20, K2tog, K24, K2tog tbl, K to end. *66 sts*
Row 36 P.
Row 37 K20, K2tog, K22, K2tog tbl, K to end. *64 sts*
Row 38 P.

First cheek
Row 1 Cast off 2 sts, K17, turn. *18 sts*
Row 2 Cast off 2 sts, P15, turn. *16 sts*
Row 3 Cast off 3 sts, K12, turn. *13 sts*
Row 4 Cast off 3 sts, K9, turn. *10 sts*
Rep last 2 rows once more.
Cast off remaining 4 sts.

Second cheek
Slip central 24 sts onto a stitch holder.
Re-join yarn and work the second cheek as for the first cheek.

Back of head
Slip the central sts back onto the needles and re-join the yarn so that the first row is a RS row.
Row 1 K2tog, K to last 2 sts, K2tog tbl. *22 sts*
Row 2 P.
Rep last 2 rows until 2 sts remain.
K2tog and fasten off.

EARS (make 2)
Outer ear
Using 4mm (US 6) needles and MC, cast on 5 sts.
Row 1 K1, M1 into next 2 sts, K2. *7 sts*
Row 2 P2, M1 into next 2 sts, P3. *9 sts*
Row 3 M1 into first st, K6, M1 into next st, K1. *11 sts*

Row 4 M1 into first st, P8, M1 into next st, P1. *13 sts*
Row 5 K1, [M1, K2] to end of row. *17 sts*
Work 7 rows in st st.
Row 13 Skpo twice, K9, K2tog twice.
Row 14 P.
Row 15 Skpo, K7, K2tog, K2. *11 sts*
Row 16 P.
Row 17 Skpo, K1, K3tog, K1, K2tog, K2. *7 sts*
Row 18 P.
Cast off.

Inner ear (knitted version)
Work as for outer ear but using 3.5mm (US 4) needles and pink yarn.

BODY AND LEGS
Body (make 2)
Using 4mm (US 6) needles and MC, cast on 4 sts.
Row 1 (RS) M1 into every st. *8 sts*
Row 2 and every alt row P.
Row 3 M1 into every st. *16 sts*
Row 5 Inc 1 st at each end of row. *18 sts*
Work 15 rows in st st.
Place stitch marker or coloured yarn at each end of last row.
Rows 21 & 23 Inc 1 st at each end of row. *22 sts*
Work 15 rows in st st.
***Row 39 & 41** Inc 1 st at each end of row. *26 sts*
Work 5 rows in st st. *
Rep from * to * once more. *30 sts*
Work 2 rows in st st.
Slip the first 15 sts onto a stitch holder and the second 15 sts onto another stitch holder.
Work the second side of the body.

Legs
Slip the second set of 15 sts from the second side of the body onto the needle. Then slip the first set of 15 sts from the first side of the body onto the needle. *30 sts*
Beg with a K row, work 80 rows in st st.
****Row 1 (RS)** K6, M1 into next st, K to end. *31 sts*
Next and every alt row P.
Row 3 K6, M1 into next 2 sts, K to end. *33 sts*
Row 5 K7, M1 into next 2 sts, K to end. *35 sts*
Row 7 K8, M1 into next 2 sts, K to end. *37 sts*
Row 9 K9, M1 into next 2 sts, K to end. *39 sts*
Row 10 P.

For the mouse with knitted feet, break off MC and join in the pink yarn; for the mouse with the fabric feet, continue with MC.

Row 11 K9, K2tog, K1, K2tog tbl, K12, K2tog, K1, K2tog tbl, K to end. *35 sts*

Row 13 K8, K2tog, K1, K2tog tbl, K10, K2tog, K1, K2tog tbl, K to end. *31 sts*

Row 15 K7, K2tog, K1, K2tog tbl, K8, K2tog, K1, K2tog tbl, K to end. *27 sts*

Row 16 P.

Cast off.

Slip the remaining set of sts onto the needles (ensuring the seam is on the inside of the leg) and work as first leg to **.

Then work second foot as follows:

Row 1 (RS) K23, M1 into next st, K to end. *31 sts*

Next and every alt row P.

Row 3 K22, M1 into next 2 sts, K to end. *33 sts*

Row 5 K23, M1 into next 2 sts, K to end. *35 sts*

Row 7 K24, M1 into next 2 sts, K to end. *37 sts*

Row 9 K25, M1 into next 2 sts, K to end. *39 sts*

Row 10 P.

For the mouse with knitted feet, break off MC and join in the pink yarn; for the mouse with the fabric feet, continue with MC.

Row 11 K8, K2tog, K1, K2tog tbl, K12, K2tog, K1, K2tog tbl, K to end. *35 sts*

Row 13 K7, K2tog, K1, K2tog tbl, K10, K2tog, K1, K2tog tbl, K to end. *31 sts*

Row 15 K6, K2tog, K1, K2tog tbl, K8, K2tog, K1, K2tog tbl, K to end. *27 sts*

Row 16 P.

Cast off.

ARMS (make 2)

Using 4mm (US 6) needles and MC, cast on 4 sts.

Row 1 (RS) M1 into every st. *8 sts*

Row 2 and every alt row P.

Row 3 M1 into every st. *16 sts*

Row 5 Inc 1 st at each end of row. *18 sts*

Work 15 rows in st st.

Place stitch marker or coloured yarn at each end of the last row.

Work another 16 rows in st st.

Row 37 (RS) K2tog to end of row. *9 sts*

Work 3 rows in st st.

Row 41 M1 into every st. *18 sts*

Work 11 rows in st st.

Row 53 K2tog to end of row. *9 sts*

Row 54 [P2tog] 4 times, P1.

Thread yarn through remaining 5 sts and fasten off.

TAIL

With 4mm (US 6) double-pointed needles and MC, cast on 4 sts and make an I-cord thus:

K to end of row.

*Slide the sts to the right-hand end of the needle.

Pull yarn taut and K another row. *

Rep from * to * until the 'tail' is 10cm long.

Next row K2, M1 into next st, K1. *5 sts*

Cont I-cord for another 10cm.

Next row K2, M1 into next st, K2. *6 sts*

Cont I-cord for another 10cm.

Next row K3, M1 into next st, K2. *7 sts*

Cont I-cord for another 10cm.

Discontinue I-cord and work 3 rows in st st.

Cast off.

TO MAKE UP

Block and press work.

Join the inside leg seams together.

Join the head seams together.

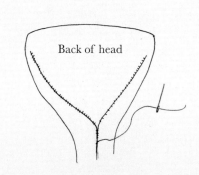

Back of head

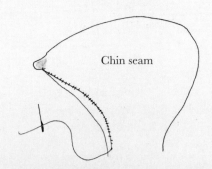

Chin seam

Using small running sts, gather the neck edge. Stuff the head.

Using mattress st and beg at the toe, join the foot seams and cont joining the inside leg seams; halfway up the inside leg, stuff the feet and lower legs. Join the rest of the leg seams and stuff.

Using mattress st, join the body as far as the stitch markers, stuff the lower body. Using mattress st, join the hand and arm seams, stuff the hand and the lower arm. Join the rem arm and body seams together. Stuff the upper arms and the body. Gather the neck opening and fasten off.

Sew the head to the body, making sure the nose and the feet face the same way.

With small running stitches, work a circle around the midpoint of the face, pull yarn taught to form a button nose.

Make indentations for the eyes by sewing a piece of yarn right through the front of the face through the eye socket position. Using dark yarn, embroider eyes by making a small circle in chain stitch or sew a black bead or button into place.

If using the knitted inner ears: place the inner and outer ears together with WS together and sew together using mattress st.

For the fabric-lined ears: Using the guide, cut the two inner ear shapes, place the fabric inner ear and the knitted outer ear together with RS together and sew all around, leaving a slit at the base of the ear. Turn to the RS and press.

For both variations: Fold the ears in two so that the lower part forms a V and sew to the head. Form whiskers by taking the yarn through the nose and tying a knot both side.

For fabric feet: Draw around the foot guide, place the fabric onto a piece of embroidery stabiliser and satin stitch all around the marked edge. Cut away the excess fabric and pull the stabiliser away. Sew the foot pads into place.

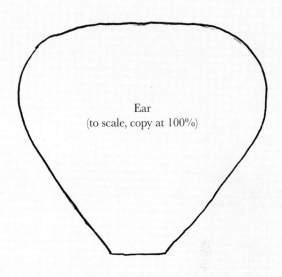

Ear
(to scale, copy at 100%)

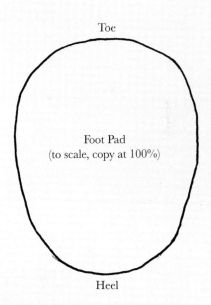

Toe

Foot Pad
(to scale, copy at 100%)

Heel

Mice Clothes

Glamis Mouse Dress

FRONT BODICE
With 4mm needles and CC, cast on 32 sts.
K 2 rows.
Beg with a K row, work 3 rows in st st.
Row 6 K.
Change to MC and st st.
Work 6 rows.
Cast off 3 sts at beg of next 2 rows. *26 sts*
Row 15 K2tog, K to last 2 sts, K2tog. *24 sts*
Row 16 P.
Rep last 2 rows once more. *22 sts*
Work 14 rows in st st.

Divide for neck and shoulders – work each shoulder
separately.
First shoulder
Row 1 (RS) K8, turn.
Row 2 P2tog, P to end. *7 sts*
Row 3 K to last 2 sts, K2tog. *6 sts*
Cast off these 6 sts.

Second shoulder
Row 1 Slip first 6 sts (neck) onto a safety pin,
re-join yarn, K2tog, K to end. *7 sts*
Row 2 P to the last 2 sts, P2tog. *6 sts*
Row 3 K.
Cast off.

BACK

With 4mm (US 6) needles and CC, cast on 32 sts.
K 2 rows.
Beg with a K row, work 3 rows in st st.
Row 6 K.

Divide for back opening
Back right piece

Change to MC, K16, turn and work on these 16 sts
only, leaving rem sts on a stitch holder.
Row 2 K1, P to end.
Row 3 K.
Rep last 2 rows once more.
Row 6 K1, P to end.
Row 7 Cast off 3 sts, K to end. *13 sts*
Row 8 K1, P to last 2 sts, P2tog. *12 sts*
Row 9 K2tog, K to end. *11sts*
Row 10 K1, P to end.
Row 11 K.
Row 12 K1, P to end.
Rep last 2 rows 6 times more.
Row 25 (RS) K6, turn.
Row 26 P.
Row 27 K6, turn.
Cast off these 6 sts.
Slip remaining 5 sts onto a safety pin.

Back left piece

Re-join yarn to rem 16 sts on stitch holder.
Row 1 (RS) K.
Row 2 P to last st, K1.
Rep last 2 rows twice more.
Row 7 K to last 2 sts, K2tog. *15 sts*
Row 8 Cast off 3 sts, P to last st, K1. *12 sts*
Row 9 K to last 2 sts, K2tog. *11 sts*
Row 10 P to last st, K1.
Row 11 K.
Rep last 2 rows 6 times more.
Row 24 P6, turn.
Row 25 K.
Rep last 2 rows once more.
Cast off these 6 sts.
Slip remaining 5 sts onto a safety pin.

Using 4mm (US 6) needles and MC, cast on 46 sts.
Work 8 rows in st st, knitting 1 st at each end of every
P row.
**

Row 1 (RS) K.
Row 2 K40, wrap, turn.
Row 3 and every alt row K to the bottom edge
unless otherwise stated.
Row 4 K35, wrap, turn.
Row 6 K30, wrap, turn.
Row 8 K25, wrap, turn.
Row 10 K20, wrap, turn.
Row 12 K15, wrap, turn.
Row 14 K10, wrap, turn.
Row 16 K5, wrap, turn.
Row 17 K to the bottom edge.
Row 18 K to the top edge, picking up all the wrap sts
as described.
Row 19 K to the bottom edge.
Row 20 K5, wrap, turn.
Row 22 K10 picking up the last wrap, wrap, turn.
Row 24 K15 picking up the last wrap, wrap, turn.
Row 26 K20 picking up the last wrap, wrap, turn.
Row 28 K25 picking up the last wrap, wrap, turn.
Row 30 K30 picking up the last wrap, wrap, turn.
Row 32 K35 picking up the last wrap, wrap, turn.
Row 34 K40 picking up the last wrap, wrap, turn.
Row 35 K to the bottom edge.
Row 36 K to the top edge, picking up the last wrap.
Row 37 K to the bottom edge.
Work 15 rows in st st, knitting 1 st at each end of every
P row and ending on a WS row. **
Rep from ** to ** twice more.
Rep Rows 1–37 once more.
Work 8 rows in st st, knitting 1 st at each end of every
P row.

BOTTOM EDGE

With 4mm (US 6) needles, RS facing and CC, pick up
and K 1 st into every row end.
Cast off loosely.

ARMHOLE EDGES

Join shoulder seams.
With 4mm (US 6) needles, RS facing, CC and beg at
underarm, pick up and K 1 st into every st and row
end around the armhole.
Cast off loosely.

NECK EDGE

With 4mm (US 6) needles, RS facing, CC and beg at
the right back neck edge, K5 sts from safety pin, pick

up and K 4 sts up to shoulder seam, pick up and K 5 sts from seam to front safety pin, K6 sts from safety pin, pick up and K 5 sts up to second shoulder seam, pick up and K 4 sts from seam to safety pin, K5 sts from final safety pin. *34 sts*
Cast off.

BOW
With 4mm (US 6) needles and CC, cast on 5 sts.
Next row Sl 1, K to end.
Repeat this row 15 times more.
Cast off.

TO MAKE UP
Join the side seams of the bodice.
Join the back seam of the skirt leaving a gap for the tail.
Sew the skirt to the bodice.
Make 4 button loops on the central edge of the back left piece (see page 121).
Sew buttons on back right piece to correspond with the button loops.
Twist and gather centre of the bow and sew into place

Glamis Mouse Jacket

You will need

YARN
Rooster *Almerino DK*
1 x 50g/1¾oz ball *(Grape)*

NEEDLES
Pair of 4mm (US 6) knitting needles

EXTRAS
Buttons: 1 x 11mm/²⁄₄in button for covering
Fabric: 72cm x 2.5cm/28¼ x 2in of bias binding
1 snap fastener
Matching sewing thread

TENSION
21 sts and 38 rows to 10cm/4in square over garter st using 4mm (US 6) needles

NOTE
Work in garter st throughout.

JACKET
Back
With 4mm (US 6) needles, cast on 30 sts.
Work 10 rows straight.
Next row K13, cast off 4 sts, K to end.
Next row K13, cast on 4 sts, K to end.
Work straight until back measures 12cm/4¾in.

Increase for sleeves
Next row Inc 1 st into the first st, K to last 2 sts, inc into next st, K1. *32 sts*
Rep last row 5 times more. *42 sts*
Cast on 10 sts at the end of the next 2 rows. *62 sts*
Work straight until back measures 21cm/8¼in, ending on a WS row.

Divide for fronts
Next row K26, cast off 10 sts, K to end.
Work each front separately.
Row 1 K to last 2 sts (neck edge), K2tog. *25 sts*
Row 2 K2tog, K to end. *24 sts*
Rep last 2 rows once more. *22 sts*
Work 4 rows straight.
Row 9 K to last 2 sts, inc 1 st into next st, K1. *23 sts*
Row 10 K1, inc 1 st into next st, K to end. *24 sts*
Rep last 2 rows, inc 1 st at neck edge on every row, 4 times more. *32 sts*
Work straight until work measures 26.5cm/10½in from cast-on edge, ending at the armhole edge.
Next row Cast off 10 sts, K to end. *22 sts*
Dec 1 st at armhole edge on every row until 15 sts remain.
Work straight until front measures the same as back.
Cast off.

With RS facing, re-join yarn at neck edge and K to end. *26 sts*
Work the second side the same as the first side from Row 1.

TO MAKE UP
Block and press work.
Join the sleeve seams, inverting the end of the sleeve seam.

With RSs facing, sew the bias binding all around the front and neck edge. Fold the bias binding to the inside and slip st into position.

Sew a snap fastener to the top of the gilet so that the right front overlaps the left front.

Sew a covered button to the top right front over the snap fastener.

Hampton Mouse Jumper

You will need

YARN

Rowan *Pure Wool 4ply*
1 x 50g/1³/₄oz ball in main colour *(Navy)* and a small amount in white for the mouse

NEEDLES

Pair of 3.25mm (US 3) knitting needles
Stitch holder

EXTRAS

Buttons: 4 x 15mm/²/₄in buttons

TENSION

28 sts and 36 rows to 10cm/4in square over st st using 3.25mm (US 3) needles

BACK

With 3.25mm (US 3) needles and MC, cast 34 sts.
Work 6 rows in moss st.
Work 2 rows in st st.
Next row K14, cast off 6 sts (for tail slit), K to end.
Next row P14, cast on 6 sts, P to end.
Cont in st st until the back measures 9cm/3½in.
Mark each end of next row.
Cont in st st until back measures 16cm/6¼in, ending on a WS row.

Shape neck

Next row K10, turn and work on these sts only.
Work 2 rows in st st.
Cast off.

Slip centre 14 sts (neck sts) onto a safety pin.
With RS facing, re-join yarn to left shoulder at neck edge and work 3 rows in st st.
Cast off.

FRONT

With 3.25mm (US 3) needles and MC, cast 34 sts.
Work 6 rows in moss st .
Work 2 rows in st st.
Next row K2, ioin in CC and using the intarsia method, work Row 1 of the mouse motif chart (see page 110), K14.
Next row P14, work Row 2 of mouse chart, P2.
Cont in this way until all 19 rows of the chart have been worked.
With MC only, cont in st st until front measures 9cm/3½in.
Mark each end of next row.
Cont in st st until front measures 15cm/6in, ending on a WS row.

Shape neck

Next row Work 13 sts, turn and work on these sts only.
Next row K2tog (neck edge), work to end. *12 sts*
Next row Work to neck edge.
Rep last 2 rows twice more. *10 sts*
Cast off.

Slip centre 8 sts (neck sts) onto a safety pin.
With RS facing, re-join yarn to right shoulder at neck edge and work right shoulder as the left, reversing shaping.

SLEEVES

With 3.25mm (US 3) needles and MC, cast 26 sts.
Work 6 rows in moss st.
Change to st st and inc 1 st at each end of next and every foll 4ᵗʰ row until there are 42 sts.

Cont straight in st st until sleeve measures
15cm/6in.
Cast off.

TO MAKE UP

Block and press work.
Join the very end of the shoulder seams (armhole
edge) with a couple of sts.
Fold the sleeves in two and marry the fold with
the shoulder seams.
Using the markers as a guide, sew the sleeves
into position.
Join the side and sleeve seams.
Form 2 loops on each shoulder to act as
buttonholes (see page 123).
Sew the buttons to correspond with the loops.

Front neck band

With 3.25mm (US 3) needles, MC and RS facing,
pick up and K 6 sts from left front neck, K8 from
front safety pin, pick up and K 6 sts from right
front neck. *20 sts*
Work 4 rows in moss st.
Cast off.

Back neck band

With 3.25mm (US 3) needles, MC and RS facing,
pick up and K 3 sts from left back neck, K14 from
back safety pin, pick up and K 3 sts from right
back neck. *20 sts*
Work 4 rows in moss st.
Cast off.

Ear

With 3.25mm (US 3) needles and CC, cast on
3 sts.
Row 1 K.
Row 2 P.
Next row K2tog, slip last st back onto the left-
hand needle, K2tog tbl.
Fasten off.

TAIL

With 2.75mm (US 2) double-pointed needles, cast
on 2 sts and work an I-cord thus:
K to end of row.
*Slide the sts to the right-hand side of the needle.
Pull yarn taut and K another row. *
Rep from * to * until the 'tail' is 12cm/4¾in long.
Next row K2tog and fasten off.

Sew the ear into place.
Sew a bead or form a French knot (see page 122)
for the eye.
Sew the tail into place and arrange as required.
Sew a pink French knot for the nose.

CHART

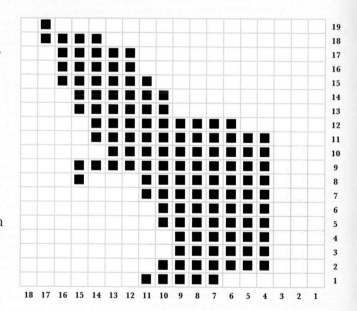

Key

RS: Knit
WS: Purl

Main colour

Contrast colour

Hampton Mouse Fabric Trousers

Copy the pattern opposite, using a home printer
or photocopier.
Fold the fabric in two and place the pattern,
making sure the straight grain line is on the
straight grain of the fabric. Pin and cut out.
With a zig-zag stitch, sew all around the edges of
each piece to prevent fraying.
Join the side seams (marked A on the pattern).
Join the back seam, leaving a gap in the seam for
the tail (marked B on the pattern).
Snip the curve so that the seam lays flat.

Snip the top of the seams under the crotch area.
Press.
Turn the waist edge down approx 1cm/½in and
sew to form a casing.
Turn the bottom of the legs under and sew
into place.
Press.
Run a piece of hat elastic through the
waist casing.

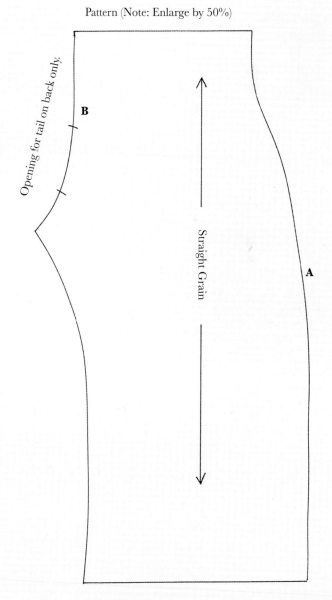

Pattern (Note: Enlarge by 50%)

Opening for tail on back only.

B

Straight Grain

A

Press seam open.
Join and press the front seam.
Pin the 2 inner seams together under the crotch
area, then pin and sew the inner leg seams.

Kensington Mouse Dress

You will need

YARN
Rooster *Baby Rooster*
Small amount of main colour
(Parma Violet)
Small amount of contrast colour
(Vintage Rose)

NEEDLES
Pair each of 3mm (US 2/3) and 3.25mm
(US 3) knitting needles

EXTRAS
Buttons: 2 x 10mm/²/₄in button
Fabric: 90cm/35in wide x 28cm/11in long.
Muslin: 90cm/35in wide x 21cm/8¼in
long after washing

TENSION
25 sts and 34 rows to 10cm/4in square
over st st using 3.25mm (US 3) needles

FRONT BODICE
With 3.25mm (US 3) needles and CC, cast on 34 sts.
K 2 rows.
Beg with a K row, work 4 rows in st st.
Row 7 (RS) P.
Row 8 K.
Change to MC and beg with K row, work 2 rows in
st st.
Cast off 3 sts at beg of next 2 rows. *28 sts*
Dec 1 st at beg of every row until 24 sts remain. **
Work straight in st st until front measures 5cm/2in,
ending on a WS row.

Divide for neck and shoulders
Row 1 K10, cast off 4 sts, K to end.

Right shoulder (work each shoulder separately)
Row 2 P.
Row 3 K2tog, K to end. *9 sts*
Rep last 2 rows until 6 sts remain.
Next row P.
Cast off.

Left shoulder
With WS facing, re-join yarn at neck edge and P
to end.
Work as for right shoulder, reversing shaping.

BACK
Work as for Front to **.
Work straight until front measures 6cm/2¼in, end-
ing on a WS row.
Next row K6, cast off 12 sts, K to end.
Work each shoulder separately, by working straight
until armhole measures the same as the front armhole,
ending on a WS row.
Cast off.

BOW
With 3.25mm (US 3) needles and CC, cast on 5 sts.
Next row Sl 1, K to end.
Rep last row until bow measures 8cm/3¼in.
Cast off.

TO MAKE UP
Block and press work.
Join both side seams.

Bands
Back neck band
With RS facing, 3mm (US 2/3) needles, MC and beg
at the inside right back shoulder, pick up and K into
every st up to the inside left back shoulder.
Cast off.

Front neck band
Work as for Back, beg at the inside left front shoulder.
Cast off.

Armhole bands
Right armhole band
With RS facing, 3mm (US 2/3) needles, MC and beg
at the front outside shoulder, pick up and K into every
st up to the back outside shoulder.
Cast off.

Left armhole band

Work as for Right, beg at the back outside shoulder.
Cast off.
Make a loop on each of the back shoulders to act as buttonholes (see page 123).

Skirt

Follow the making up instructions for the Long-Sleeved Dress (see page 29-31) and join to the bodice using 90 x 28cm/35²/₄ x 11in of fabric and 90 x 21cm/35²/₄ x 8¹/₄in of pre-washed muslin. Do not at this point sew the slit in the lining together.

Try dress on mouse and sew buttons in the correct position.
Locate the position of the tail and, with a stitch un-picker, make a slit in the seam for the tail.
Over-sew each side of the slit to prevent tearing.
Sew the opening in the lining together, sewing around the tail slit.
Twist and gather centre of the bow and sew into place.

HEADBAND

With 3.25 (US 3) needles and CC, cast on 75 sts.
K 2 rows.
Beg with a K row, work 3 rows in st st.
K 2 rows.
Cast off.

Bow

Make bow as for dress.

TO MAKE UP

Block and press headband.
Place the band around the mouse's head and over-lap the ends to form a snug fit, sew into place.
Twist and gather centre of the bow and sew into place on to the overlap.

Holyrood Mouse Jumper

You will need

YARN
Millamia *Naturally Soft Merino*
1 x 50g/1³/₄oz balls for main colour
(Forget Me Not)
Small amount of contrasting colour
(Midnight)

NEEDLES
Pair of 3.25mm (US 3) knitting needles

EXTRAS
Buttons: 6 x 15mm/²/₄in button
Stitch holder

TENSION
24 sts and 34 rows to 10cm/4in square over moss st using 3.25mm (US 3) needles

ABBREVIATIONS

C2B – cable two back – slip next 2 sts onto a cable needle and hold at back of the work, K2, K2 from cable needle
C2F – cable two front – slip next 2 sts onto a cable needle and hold at front of the work, K2, K2 from cable needle

BACK

With 3.25mm (US3) needles and CC, cast 34 sts.
K 1 row.
Change to MC and work 5 rows in K1, P1 rib.
Next row Moss st 11, P2, K8, P2, moss st to end.
Next row Moss st 11, K2, P8, K2, moss st to end.
Next row Moss st 11, P2, K1, cast off 6 sts (for tail slit), P2, moss st to end.
Next row Moss st 11, K2, P1, cast on 6 sts, P1, K2, moss st to end.
Row 1 Moss st 11, P2, K8, P2, moss st to end.
Row 2 Moss st 11, K2, P8, K2, moss st to end.
Row 3 Moss st 11, P2, C2F, C2B, P2, moss st to end.
Row 4 Moss st 11, K2, P8, K2, moss st to end.

Row 5 Moss st 11, P2, K8, P2, moss st to end.
Row 6 Moss st 11, K2, P8, K2, moss st to end.
Row 7 Moss st 11, P2, C2B, C2F, P2, moss st to end.
Row 8 Moss st 11, K2, P8, K2, moss st to end.
Rows 1 to 8 form the cable pattern.
Work in cable pattern until the back measures
9cm/3½in.
Mark each end of next row.
Cont in pattern until back measures 16cm/6¼in,
ending on a WS row.

Neck shaping
Next row Moss st 10, turn and work on these sts only.
Work 2 rows in moss st.
Cast off.

Slip centre 14 sts (neck sts) onto a safety pin.
Re-join yarn to left shoulder sts at neck edge.
Work 3 rows in moss st.
Cast off.

FRONT
With 3.25mm (US 3) needles and CC, cast 34 sts.
K1 row.
Change to MC and work 5 rows in K1, P1 rib.

Work in cable pattern (as set out in Rows 1 to 8 for
the back) until the front measures 9cm/3½in.
Mark each end of next row.
Cont in cable pattern until front measures 15cm/6in,
ending with a WS row.

Neck shaping
Next row Work 13 sts, turn and work on these
sts only.
Next row K2tog (neck edge), work to end. *12 sts*
Next row Work to neck edge.
Rep last 2 rows twice more. *10 sts*
Cast off

Slip centre 8 sts (neck sts) onto a safety pin.
Re-join yarn to right shoulder sts at neck edge.
Work right shoulder as the left, reversing shaping.

SLEEVES
With 3.25mm (US 3) needles and CC, cast 26 sts.
K 1 row.
Change to MC and work 5 rows in K1, P1 rib.

Next row Moss st 7, P2, K8, P2, moss st to end.
Next row Moss st 7, K2, P8, K2, moss st to end.
Cont in pattern working the central cable as for the
back, with 7 moss sts either side.
AT THE SAME TIME, inc 1 st at each end of
next and every foll 4th row until there are 42 sts on
the needle.
Work straight in pattern until sleeve measures
15cm/6in.
Cast off.

SHOULDER PADS (make 2)
First half of shoulder pad
With 3.25mm (US 3) needles and CC, cast on 12 sts.
K 2 rows.
Next row K to last 3 sts, P1, K1, P1.
Next row K1, P1, K1, P to last 2 sts, K2tog. *11 sts*
Rep last 2 rows until 6 sts remain.
Cast off.

Second half of shoulder pad
With 3.25mm (US 3) needles and CC, cast on 12 sts
K 2 rows.
Next row P1, K1, P1, K to end.
Next row K2tog, P to last 3 sts, K1, P1, K1.
Rep last 2 rows until 6 sts remain.
Cast off.

TO MAKE UP
Block and press work.
Join the very end of the shoulder seams (at armhole)
with a couple of sts.
Fold the sleeves in two and marry the fold with the
shoulder seams.
Using the markers as a guide, sew the sleeves into
position.
Join the side and sleeve seams.
Sew the shoulder pads into position so that the front
over laps the back by approx. 0.5cm/¼in.
Form 2 loops on each shoulder to act as buttonholes
(see page 123).
Sew the buttons to correspond with the loops.

Front neck band
With 3.25 (US 3) needles, MC and RS facing, pick up
and K 6 sts from left front neck, K8 from front safety
pin, pick up and K 6 sts from right front neck. *20 sts*
Work 3 rows in K1, P1 rib.
Change to CC and K 1 row.
Cast off.

Back neck band

With 3.25 (US 3) needles, MC and RS facing, pick up and K 3 sts from right back neck, K14 from back safety pin, pick up and K 3 sts from left back neck. Work 3 rows in K1, P1 rib.
Change to CC and K 1 row.
Cast off.

Holyrood Mouse Trousers

You will need

YARN
Millamia *Naturally Soft Merino*
1 x 50g/1¾oz balls *(midnight)*

NEEDLES
3.25mm (US 3) and 4mm (US 6) knitting needles.

TENSION
20 sts and 30 rows to 10cm/4in square over st st using 4mm (US 6) needles

LEGS (make 2)
With 4mm (US 6) needles, cast on 40 sts.
K 6 rows.
Change to st st and work 38 rows straight.

Inc 1 st at each end of next row. *42 sts*
Next row P.
Rep last 2 rows twice more. *46 sts*

Next row (RS) K3, K2tog tbl, K to last 5 sts, K2tog, K3. *44 sts*
Next row K1, P to last st, K1.

Rep last 2 rows until 32 sts remain.
Place these 32 sts onto a spare needle and complete the second leg.

With RS facing, slip both sets of sts onto a 3.25mm (US 3) needle.

Work 10 rows in K1, P1 rib.
Cast off in rib.

TO MAKE UP
Block and press work.
Using mattress st, join the front seam (in the centre of the work).
Join the back seam leaving a gap for the tail.
Join the leg seams.

Size Diagrams

The size diagrams show the width and length of the finished garments.

Glamis

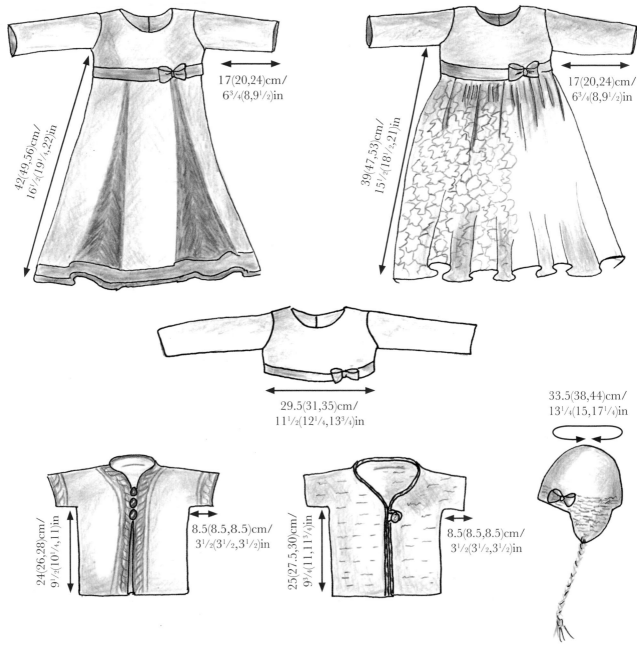

17(20,24)cm/
6³/₄(8,9¹/₂)in

42(49,56)cm/
16¹/₂(19¹/₄,22)in

39(47,53)cm/
15¹/₂(18¹/₂,21)in

17(20,24)cm/
6³/₄(8,9¹/₂)in

29.5(31,35)cm/
11¹/₂(12¹/₄,13³/₄)in

33.5(38,44)cm/
13¹/₄(15,17¹/₄)in

24(26,28)cm/
9¹/₂(10¹/₄,11)in

8.5(8.5,8.5)cm/
3¹/₂(3¹/₂,3¹/₂)in

25(27.5,30)cm/
9³/₄(11,11³/₄)in

8.5(8.5,8.5)cm/
3¹/₂(3¹/₂,3¹/₂)in

Hampton

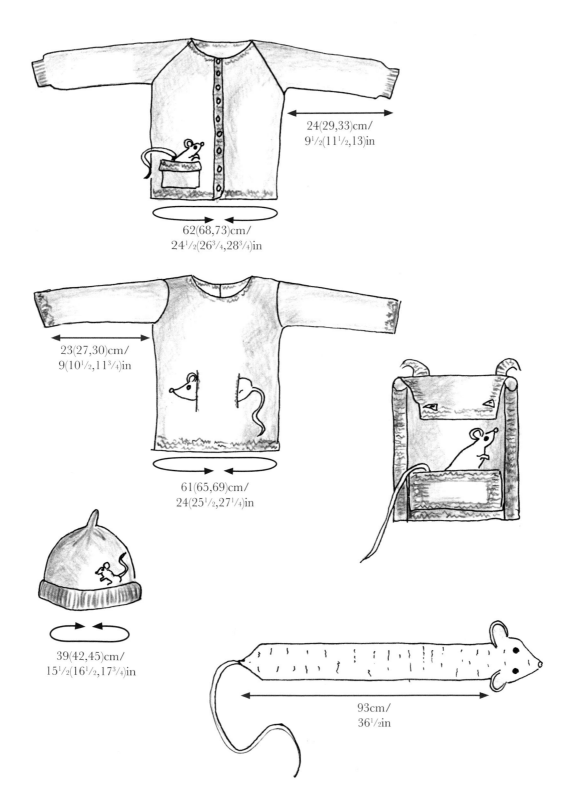

24(29,33)cm/
9^1/$_2$(11^1/$_2$,13)in

62(68,73)cm/
24^1/$_2$(26^3/$_4$,28^3/$_4$)in

23(27,30)cm/
9(10^1/$_2$,11^3/$_4$)in

61(65,69)cm/
24(25^1/$_2$,27^1/$_4$)in

39(42,45)cm/
15^1/$_2$(16^1/$_2$,17^3/$_4$)in

93cm/
36^1/$_2$in

Kensington

39(47,53)cm/
15½(18½,21)in

39(47,53)cm/
15½(18½,21)in

19(22,24)cm/
7½(8¾,9½)in

12(14.5,17)cm/
4¾(5¾,6¾)in

60(63,66)cm/
23½(24¾,26)in

One Size
fits 34-56cm/
13½-22in

19(22,24)cm/
7½(8¾,9½)in

13(14,15)cm/
5¼(5½,6)in

60(63,66)cm/
23½(24¾,26)in

19(22,24)cm/
7½(8¾,9½)in

25(27.5,30)cm/
9¾(11,11¾)in

Holyrood

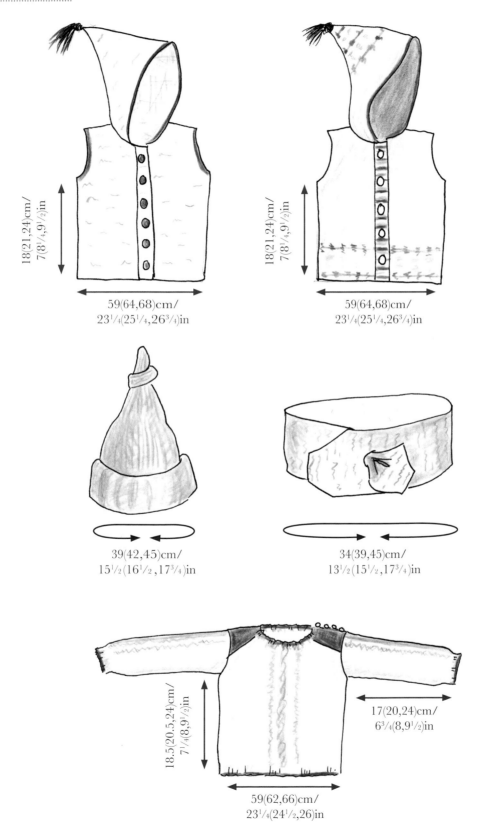

18(21,24)cm/
7(8¹⁄₄,9¹⁄₂)in

59(64,68)cm/
23¹⁄₄(25¹⁄₄,26³⁄₄)in

18(21,24)cm/
7(8¹⁄₄,9¹⁄₂)in

59(64,68)cm/
23¹⁄₄(25¹⁄₄,26³⁄₄)in

39(42,45)cm/
15¹⁄₂(16¹⁄₂,17³⁄₄)in

34(39,45)cm/
13¹⁄₂(15¹⁄₂,17³⁄₄)in

18.5(20.5,24)cm/
7¹⁄₄(8,9¹⁄₂)in

17(20,24)cm/
6³⁄₄(8,9¹⁄₂)in

59(62,66)cm/
23¹⁄₄(24¹⁄₂,26)in

Finishing Touches

To make garments look extra special, little finishing touches add that finesse that can really set your finished project apart.

Covered Buttons

Knitted covered buttons

Place the button in the centre on the WS of the knitted square (A).

Using small running stitches and strong thread, gather around the button and pull thread tight, fasten off (B).

Sew a couple of stitches through the centre of the button to keep the covering in place (C).

Make a 'stalk' on the underside of the button by wrapping thread around the base (D).

Fabric covered buttons

Cut 3, 15mm/½in circles from the fabric. Using strong thread, run stitches around the edge of the circle (A).

Wet the fabric, place the button in the middle of the circle and gather the stitches (B).

Press the washer into place (a small cotton reel pressed on the stalk of the button will help to make the washer even) (C).

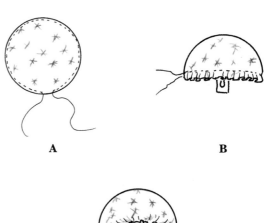

A

B

C

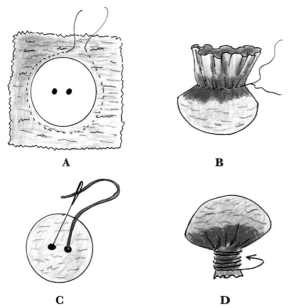

A

B

C

D

Bias Binding

To make bias binding

To make garments look extra special, finish by sewing a small strip of matching or contrasting bias binding to the back of the neck, this not only looks attractive and disguises the back neck seam it also make the neckline smooth and a pleasure to wear. A small piece of ribbon can be used instead but bias binding has stretch and will give a much better finish.

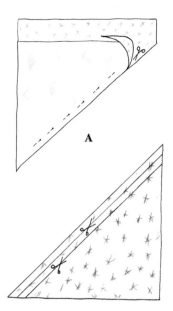

A

B

Decide what width of bias binding you want. For the back of a neck I use 12.5mm x 1cm /5 x ½in.

Fold the fabric onto itself so that selvages are at right angles to each other. Pin into place (A).

Using a ruler and tailor's chalk or a pencil, draw lines approx. double the finished width of the binding. Pin between each line to hold the fabric steady and carefully cut along the markings (B).

Join the bias strips by placing them right sides together at 90-degrees to each other.

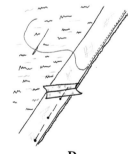

C

Sew across the join; you should have a small triangle of fabric at each end (C).

Press open. Sew your bias binding to the RS of the garment (D).

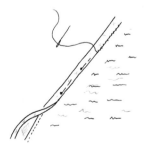

D

Turn the bias binding to the inside of the garment and slip stitch into place (E).

Although the tape can be used and folded as you go along, I recommend using a tape maker (available at any good haberdashers) for a really even finish. Just run the tape through and press with an iron (F).

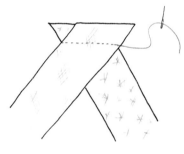

E

Lazy daisy, French knot & Stem stitch

Lazy daisy stitch

Thread a yarn needle with a length of yarn. Secure the yarn on the wrong side of the knitting and bring it up at the centre of the flower. Take the needle back down at the starting point and out again at the edge of the flower, creating a loop, as shown. Secure the loop with a short stitch. Repeat to make all the petals, starting at the same central point.

French knot

1 Thread a yarn needle with a length of yarn. Bring the needle out where the knot is required and wrap the yarn around the needle twice.

2 Push the wraps against the fabric, holding them in place with your thumb, and re-insert the needle next to where the yarn emerges.

3 Hold the knot against the fabric and take the yarn through to the back, leaving the knot in place.

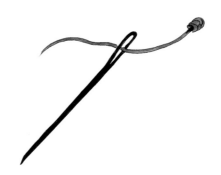

Stem stitch

1 Bring out the thread through point A and take it in through point B. Take the needle backwards and bring the thread out through point C. Make sure that point C lies over the stitch A–B.

2 Note that point C lies about half way through point A and B. Also note that point C lies on top of the stitch A–B. So, all the subsequent stitch points will lie on top their previous stitch.

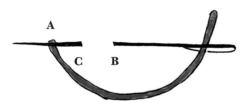

3 Take the needle in through D. Try to ensure D is spaced in a way that will have point B half way between C–D. Bring the needle out through B.

Buttonhole loops

1 Sew 3 or 4 lengths of yarn onto the opening to form a loop making sure the ends are secure.

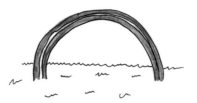

2 Blanket stitch around the loop.

3 Blanket stitch secure a long piece of yarn at the base of the loop. Take the needle under the loop, bring the needle up and around the loop making sure the yarn is behind the needle. Pull the yarn though and take it around the loop as before. Continue in this way until the whole of the loop is covered.

Abbreviations

alt	alternate
approx.	approximately
beg	begin(s)(ning)
CC	contrast colour yarn
cm	centimetres
cont	continu(e)(ing)
dec	decreas(e)(ing)
foll	follow(s)(ing)
g	gram
in	inch(es)
inc	increas(e)(ing)
K	knit
K2tog	knit next 2 stitches together
MC	main colour yarn
M1	make one stitch by picking up horizontal loop bcfore next stitch and knitting into back of it
mm	millimetres
P	purl
psso	pass slipped stitch over
P2tog	purl next 2 stitches together
rem	remain(s)(ing)
rep	repeat
rev st st	reverse stocking stitch / stockinette stitch
RS	right side
s2kpo	slip 2 stitches together, k1, pass slipped stitches over
skpo	slip 1 stitch, k1, pass slipped stitch over
sk2po	slip 1 stitch, k2tog, pass slipped stitch over
sl 1	slip one stitch
st(s)	stitch(es)
st st	stocking stitch/ stockinette stitch (1 row knit, 1 row purl)
tbl	through back of loop(s)
tog	together
WS	wrong side
yds	yards
yf	yarn forward
[ ]/*	repeat instructions within square brackets or between asterisks

Acknowledgements

First of all, a big thank you to Sharon Brant for that first visit to my studio and Sharon Northcott for setting the ball (or maybe that should read yarn) rolling. Thanks also to all the Brant family, especially Darren and Georgina; I certainly couldn't have done it without you! Another big thank you to my test knitters; Ann Cowling, Chris Holmes, Jacqui Daly and Cordelia Stocks.

Thanks also to Deb Bramham for translating my eclectic pattern style.

And last but by no means least, a huge thank you to Charlie Campbell – my son, my IT expert, my cheerer-upper and my friend.

Quail Publishing would also like to thank Search Press and their team, Katie French, Martin de la Bédoyère and Emily Adam, for making this title possible.

Susan Campbell for her devotion to the project and wonderful design work.

Deb Bramham for her thorough editing and technical checking.

And finally, Rowan Yarns, Rooster & Millamia for their yarn support on this project

Team Quail   Instagram: @Quail_Studio

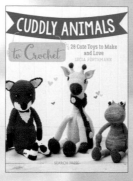

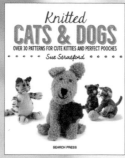

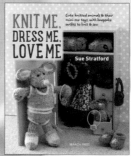